ALEXANDER BUZO

ROOTED

*un*tapped

ABOUT *UNTAPPED*

Most Australian books ever written have fallen out of print and become unavailable for purchase or loan from libraries. This includes important local and national histories, biographies and memoirs, beloved children's titles, and even winners of glittering literary prizes such as the Miles Franklin Literary Award.

Supported by funding from state and territory libraries, philanthropists and the Australian Research Council, *Untapped* is identifying Australia's culturally important lost books, digitising them, and promoting them to new generations of readers. As well as providing access to lost books and a new source of revenue for their writers, the *Untapped* collaboration is supporting new research into the economic value of authors' reversion rights and book promotion by libraries, and the relationship between library lending and digital book sales. The results will feed into public policy discussions about how we can better support Australian authors, readers and culture.

See untapped.org.au for more information, including a full list of project partners and rediscovered books.

Readers are reminded that these books are products of their time. Some may contain language or reflect views that might now be found offensive or inappropriate.

CONTENTS

CHARACTERS

BENTLEY

SANDY

GARY

RICHARD

DIANE

All the characters are in their mid-twenties.

SCENE

Sydney, over a period of ten weeks.

ACT I
The living room of BENTLEY
and SANDY's home unit.

ACT II
The same.

ACT III
RICHARD's studio.

Rooted was first performed simultaneously on 14th August 1969 by Stage at the Childers Street Hall, Canberra and at the Jane Street Theatre, Sydney, with the following casts, respectively:

BENTLEY
Bruce Widdop

SANDY
Karin Altmann

GARY
Clive Scollay

RICHARD
Philip Wheeler

DIANE
Peta Adams

Setting designed by Jon Stephens

Directed by Allan Mawer

BENTLEY
Jeff Kevin

SANDY
Pat Bishop

GARY
Gregory Ross

RICHARD
Garry McDonald

DIANE
Sandy Gore

Setting designed by Kim Carpenter

Directed by Rick Billinghurst

ACT ONE

SCENE ONE

Saturday night. The living room of BENTLEY *and* SANDY's *home unit. The room is white and all the furniture is white, except for two armchairs, which are blue. The furniture is very modern. There is a door, down R., and a passageway, up L. There is one window in the right wall upstage. There is a sideboard along the right wall, a stereo set against the back wall and a cabinet against the left wall. The walls are bare. On the sideboard there is a tape recorder, a transistor radio, and a telephone.*

BENTLEY *and* SANDY's *house-warming party has just finished and the room is littered with beer-cans, glasses, full ashtrays etc.* BENTLEY *and* SANDY *are posing for a photograph by the sideboard, and* GARY *is holding a camera. He moves around, looking for a good position.*

GARY

Say cheese.

BENTLEY

Cheese.

GARY

Got it.

BENTLEY

Let's have another one, over by the stereo set.

GARY

Righto.

BENTLEY

How's this?

(*They pose by the stereo set.*)

GARY

Say cheese.

BENTLEY

Cheese.

GARY

Got it.

BENTLEY

Let's have another one over—

SANDY

That's enough!

BENTLEY

All right, darling. Whatever you say. Like another beer, Gary?

GARY

I wouldn't mind. Just a nogginette, thanks.

(SANDY *sits down, looking tired and irritated.* BENTLEY *pours* GARY *a beer.*)

BENTLEY

Chug-a-lug.

GARY

Chug-a-lug.

BENTLEY

How did you think the turn went?

GARY

It was a beauty. Best house-warming party I've been to.

BENTLEY

What do you think of the unit?

GARY

Immaculate. Bloody immaculate.

BENTLEY

You hear that, Sandy? Gary reckons our unit's immaculate.

SANDY

Yes, I heard.

GARY

You must have paid a pretty fair price for it.

BENTLEY

Well, they're not giving them away.

GARY

You must be doing all right for yourself, Bentley.

BENTLEY

Ar, not too bad. You think everyone enjoyed themselves tonight?

GARY

Oh yeah. It was a great turn.

BENTLEY

You hear that, Sandy? Gary reckons it was a great turn.

SANDY

Yes, I heard.

GARY

Davo got stuck into the grog, didn't he?

BENTLEY

Bloody Davo. Jees I had to laugh. Nearly went off my face.

GARY

You see Davo cracking on? First bird he's had in ages.

BENTLEY

Ar well, better than his right hand, I suppose.

GARY

Old Davo certainly enjoyed himself.

BENTLEY

You hear that, Sandy? Gary reckons Davo enjoyed himself.

SANDY

Yes, I heard.

GARY

I liked the records you played tonight, Bentley.

BENTLEY

Did you?

GARY

Yeah, bloody good music.

BENTLEY

You think everyone liked the music?

GARY

Oh yeah. Diane went off her brain.

BENTLEY

Did she ever!

GARY

That's a great stereo set you got there, Bentley.

BENTLEY

You hear that, Sandy?

SANDY

Gary reckons we've got a great stereo set.

BENTLEY

Yes, I heard.

SANDY

Do you two know what time it is?

BENTLEY

(*looking at watch*) Jees, it's a quarter to three.

SANDY

That's right.

GARY

I'd better be going.

SANDY

Yes.

GARY

Getting a bit late.

SANDY

It's a quarter to three.

GARY

Yes, I heard.

BENTLEY

One for the road?

SANDY

It's getting a bit late.

GARY

I'd better be going. See you later.

(BENTLEY *opens the door.* GARY *goes over.*)

BENTLEY

Send us the photos when they're ready.

GARY

Will do. Going down the beach tomorrow?

SANDY

Goodnight, Gary.

GARY

Goodnight.

(GARY *exits.* BENTLEY *starts clearing up the room.* SANDY *sits back in the armchair and closes her eyes.*)

BENTLEY

Are you tired, darling?

SANDY

Yes. It's getting a bit late.

BENTLEY

I'm a bit buggered myself. Enjoy the party?

SANDY

Yes.

BENTLEY

Everyone had a good time, I think. Especially Simmo.

(BENTLEY *takes some glasses and ashtrays out to the kitchen on a tray. He re-enters and tidies up.*)

Everyone raved about the unit, didn't they? Mind you, this is only a stepping stone. When I get to grade ten we'll have a villa at Bayview and a cruiser at Pittwater.

(*He continues tidying up, then stops.*)

Oh, uh, by the way, darling, there was one thing I meant to say to you.

(*Pause.*)

What was it? Well, I'll tell you, darling. You see, I noticed Simmo paying you a lot of attention tonight. He left the keg twice to talk to you. So I sort of took him aside and said: 'Look, Simmo, I know you're a big mover with the birds, but Sandy's my wife, so I'd just like to sort of ... ascertain your intentions ... as it were.'

(*Pause.*)

He told me to get stuffed.

(*Pause.*)

Huh. Funny bloke, Simmo. You want to watch out for him. Still, I know there's nothing in it.

(*Pause.*)

I wouldn't get ... involved with Simmo, if I were you.

(*Pause.*)

Still, I know there's nothing in it.

(*Pause. He continues tidying up.*)

Yes, everyone had a good time tonight. Diane went off her brain.

(*He continues tidying up as he speaks.*)

Everyone raved about the unit. And the stereo set.

(*He dusts the stereo set.*)

Yes, it was a great turn.

(*He looks at* SANDY.)

Well, that's that. Ready for bed?

(SANDY *is asleep.*)

Fast asleep. Poor darling. You're worn out.

(*He looks at her.*)

You're beautiful, you know that? The blokes've always reckoned I've hit the jackpot. Especially Davo.

(*He picks her up.*)

Come on, beddy byes.

(*He carries her out.*)

Beddy byes, darling.

(*He carries her into the bedroom and closes the door.*)

FADE OUT

SCENE TWO

Sunday afternoon, one week later. BENTLEY *sits in a chair reading the Sunday paper. The audience can't see his face. There is an ironing board and an iron at the back of the room. Silence for a while, then* SANDY *rushes in, wearing a short slip and carrying a black dress. As she talks, she irons a wet spot on the dress, and puts it on later in her speech.*

SANDY

(*loudly and quickly*) This damn dress! It's still got a mark on it. I took it to the dry cleaners around the corner the other day and they said they'd get it off all right. It'd be no trouble for them, they said, have it off in no time without any trace they said. Then I came back the next day to pick it up and the spot was still there so I really got MAD and told off the old bitch something terrible. Funny looking little woman she was, too—raven hair, eyes like a hawk, and pigeon toes. Walked with a squint and spoke like a Greek—I think she was an Italian Jew with German blood. So then she asked me what the stain was and I said beer. I said I was at this party and a CREEP called Davo spilt his drink in my lap and wet me right through and caused this big stain and you haven't got it out yet, what do you mean by calling yourselves dry cleaners it's a FRAUD. I said I'm going out on Sunday night and I went to look my best so you'd better do something about it but QUICK. That's what I told the old bitch and she said you'd better speak to the manager and took me back through the curtains to the office where this real old man was sitting behind a plastic desk with an eye shade and it looked like it was her husband—I mean he had that look about him. Jet black hair falling out with glasses and a beard. SO-O-O, then I said to him you've got a nerve what do you mean by saying you're dry cleaners when you can't even get a beer stain off my dress when I've got a date on Sunday night and want to look my best. Oh yes, he said, I remember we had the same trouble with Rebecca Rosenberg's grey slack suit. BUGGER Rebecca Rosenberg's grey slack suit I said what about my little black dress I've got a date on Sunday so DO something about it. Oooo, he said with a wrinkle in his eye, have you got yourself a boyfriend. Yes I said and I'm going out with him on Sunday night so you'd better have this dress ready in time. Oooo, he said with another wrinkle what's your boyfriend like, a nice respectable fellow. Yes I said as a matter of fact he's one of my husband's best friends. Then we got down to business and he said he'd see to it personally and come back tomorrow but when I came back tomorrow it still had a stain on it so I went back and told him and he said he was sorry with a shrug. SORRY I said look sweetheart I've got a date with Simmo on Sunday and I want to look my best so get to work on it. Simmo he said well why didn't you say you had a date with Simmo I'd have seen to it personally. SO then he took it and said come back in half an hour so I came back and it was in a plastic bag and he winked at me with his glass eye and said all was well now dear. BUT I ripped it off before his very eyes and the stain was still there on the dress so I threw it back in his face. If you don't get it out I'll get Simmo on to you I said. You should have seen him MOVE. He said come back in an hour and scuttled away with the dress and when I came back he gave it to me in another plastic bag and I said no tricks and he said no it was all right now. BUT when I got home and opened the bag it still had a stain on it I could have cried. I've tried petrol, lighter fluid, metho and kero but it won't come off so I'll just have to hope Simmo doesn't notice it.

(*A car horn is heard.*)

Oh there's Simmo now. I'll have to fly. There's some corned beef in the fridge.

(*She rushes out the front door.* BENTLEY *lowers his paper and looks after her.*)

FADE OUT

SCENE THREE

Sunday afternoon, one week later. Lights up on SANDY, *who is sitting in an armchair cleaning and filing her nails. After a little while,* BENTLEY *comes in the front door. He is wearing tennis whites and carries a racquet. In his other hand he carries a small trophy. He stands, watching* SANDY. *She appears not to notice him. Silence.*

BENTLEY

We won.

(*Pause.*)

Huh. We won the doubles cup.

(*He holds up the trophy. Pause. He puts it on the sideboard.*)

They took us to five sets.

(*Pause.*)

Whew!

(*Silence.* BENTLEY *takes a tennis ball out of his pocket and bounces it up and down on his racquet. This goes on for a little while and he gets quite wrapped up in it.* SANDY *looks up and starts watching him. He keeps it going while he reaches into his pocket and brings out another ball. He gets two of them going at once. He manages this at first, but soon he is trying desperately to keep them both going. Finally, both balls fall to the floor.* BENTLEY *and* SANDY *watch the balls bounce and then roll to a standstill. Silence.* SANDY *resumes filing her nails.*)

I went for a walk this morning. Down to the beach. Very early, it was. You were still asleep. I went down to the promenade. You know the promenade? Had a squint at the old Pacific. I walked along the promenade. Just walked along to the end there, to the rocks. You know the rocks? I stood on the rocks and looked at the sea. Very fresh, what with the salty air and the sea breeze and all. The old Pacific. What an ocean! What an ocean. Sparkling. There was a bit of mist about. Not much, just a bit. Then I walked around the headland, round a bit further where it juts out. There was a small rock pool there. I discovered it, quite by accident. A small rock pool, all by itself. A bit of sea that got left behind by the tide. The water was clear, very clear. You could see the odd grain of sand on the bottom. There was no one about, so I took a quick dip in the pool. Stripped down, hopped in, splashed about, lovely. Lovely. I lay on my back and floated along. Not a ripple. You couldn't hear a sound. I floated for quite a while, till the sun came out on the water. Sparkling. Then the mist lifted and I heard voices, so I got dressed and climbed back down to the promenade. It was sunny now, people around, splashing in the sand. There was sunlight splattered all over the place. All over the sea, all over the sand, all over me. Sunlight everywhere. Sparkling. Then I came back here. You were still asleep. I looked at you. Like a baby.

(*Pause.*)

It was a beautiful walk.

(*Pause.*)

Down there by the old Pacific. It really is a magnificent ocean, you know. Goes for miles.

(*Pause.*)

I tell you what, why don't we go for a swim?

(Pause.)

Let's hop in the B and fang up to the beach. We could go up the coast and down an ale at the Arms.

*(Pause.)*f

Might bump into Davo up there. He's been known to bend an elbow at the Arms.

(Pause.)

What do you say?

(Pause.)

About this thing with Simmo, darling. You're not ... sort of ... you know ...

(Pause.)

I'd like to have a little talk to you about this thing with Simmo.

(Pause.)

Let's have a drink and talk it over, eh?

(He goes to the sideboard and brings out a large glass bowl half filled with blue liquid, the same colour as the armchairs.)

I knocked off the punch from the turn last night. Did you have any? It was put there for the birds. Sort of a female keg. Like some?

(He gets two glasses and scoops out some punch.)

There you are. Do you good.

(He drinks, then winces.)

Jees, bloody potent stuff, this. Fair knocks you. Davo tipped a bottle of Gilbey's into it. Laced it for openers. That was the secret of his success last night. She never knew what hit her.

(*Pause.*)

Go on, have a bit. Goes down well. You'll enjoy it.

(*Pause.*)

Brushes away the cobwebs.

(*Pause.*)

About this thing with Simmo ...

(*Pause.*)

I bought some new stuff on Friday. Look at this little transistor. Latest model. Japanese. I also bought a tape recorder. Beauty, isn't it? They don't give these things away, you know. I'll show you how it works.

(*He switches it on and speaks into the microphone.*)

Testing 1-2-3.

(*He switches to playback, but* SANDY'S *voice is heard on the tape.*)

SANDY'S VOICE

Why don't you shut up?

(BENTLEY'S *jaw drops. He switches off the tape recorder looks at* SANDY, *then looks at the machine. He is disconcerted.*

BENTLEY

Huh.

SANDY

Look, I tell you what.

BENTLEY

What?

SANDY

Why don't you move out? Huh? Why don't you pack up and get out?

BENTLEY

I can't.

SANDY

Why not?

BENTLEY

I live here.

SANDY

I know you live here. I've noticed you around the place from time to time. You know what you are, don't you?

BENTLEY

No.

SANDY

You're a ghost. That's what you are. You haunt this place. You haunt me. You're worse than Davo. Sometimes I wake up in the dead of the night and I can hear you moaning. It's creepy. I just don't want you around any more.

BENTLEY

But this is my home. This is my home unit.

SANDY

I know that. But why don't you find another one? Go somewhere else? I mean, I've got all sorts of things I want to do. I'm constantly on the move. But you never do anything. I mean, what do you do, you don't do anything, do you?

BENTLEY

I do ... lots of things.

SANDY

What?

(Pause.)

BENTLEY

Lots of things.

SANDY

Let me put it in simple language: I want you to move out.

BENTLEY

Let me reply to you in equally simple language, darling: your proposal constitutes a violation of the legal rights of the duly authorised tenant of the said premises.

(Pause.)

SANDY

Anyway, you're annoying Simmo. You're getting on his nerves. I'm terribly sorry, but I must ask you to shoot through at your earliest possible convenience.

BENTLEY

But I live here.

SANDY

If you say that once more, I'll throw up.

BENTLEY

Sorry, darling.

SANDY

Look, if you don't move out, I'll get Simmo on to you.

BENTLEY

You wouldn't do that. You wouldn't do that to your own husband.

(*He moves towards her.*)

Now come on, darling. You're only kidding, aren't you?

(*He tries to put his arm around her. She has resumed her nail filing and doesn't look up.*)

SANDY

Get out of it.

(BENTLEY *retreats.*)

BENTLEY

Huh. Sorry, darling, I didn't meant to ... disrupt ...

(*Pause.*)

Anyway, you can't threaten me. No sir. You can't push me around. Huh! So what if you do go and tell him. Go ahead. I'm not scared. You tell him. Boy! Try to threaten me, eh? Huh!

(*There is a knock on the door.* BENTLEY *jumps.*)

SANDY

Answer it.

BENTLEY

What?

SANDY

Answer the door.

BENTLEY

You answer it.

SANDY

What?

BENTLEY

You answer the door.

SANDY

Get over there and open that door.

BENTLEY

What do you think I am? A bloody servant? I'm the boss around here and don't you forget it.

(*Pause.*)

I'm your kingpin.

(*Pause.*)

SANDY

Open ... that ... door.

(*Pause.*)

BENTLEY

All right, I'm going. What do I care?

(*He moves towards the door.*)

Doesn't worry me. I couldn't care less.

(*He opens the door.* RICHARD *and* DIANE *come in. They are dressed very modishly. Silence.*)

RICHARD

Hello, Bentley.

BENTLEY

Say, who are you?

RICHARD

Richard. Remember?

BENTLEY

Richard?

RICHARD

From school, remember?

BENTLEY

Oh, Richard!

RICHARD

That's right.

BENTLEY

Is that you?

RICHARD

Yes.

BENTLEY

Richard from school?

RICHARD

That's me.

BENTLEY

Richard!

RICHARD

Bentley.

BENTLEY

You've changed.

RICHARD

Yes.

BENTLEY

Richard!

RICHARD

Bentley.

BENTLEY

Old Richard, eh?

RICHARD

Yes.

BENTLEY

I can't believe it.

RICHARD

It's me all right.

BENTLEY

Richard!

RICHARD AND SANDY

Bentley!

(*Pause.*)

BENTLEY

Hello, Richard.

RICHARD

Hello, Bentley.

(*Pause. He turns to* SANDY.)

Uh ... hi.

BENTLEY

Oh sorry, I forgot. This is my wife Sandy.

(BENTLEY *turns to* SANDY.)

This is Richard.

SANDY

Who?

RICHARD

How do you do?

SANDY

How do you do.

RICHARD

You know Diane.

BENTLEY

Hello, Diane.

DIANE

Hi.

(*Pause.*)

BENTLEY

Well, what a surprise!

RICHARD

Yes.

(*Pause.*)

BENTLEY

Haven't seen you for years.

RICHARD

No, must be ... well, not since we left school.

(*They smile awkwardly at each other.*)

BENTLEY

What are you doing with yourself these days?

RICHARD

Oh, nothing much. What about you?

BENTLEY

Oh, I'm with the public service. Been there for years. Grade three now. Alan White reckons I'm a moral for grade four.

RICHARD

Yeah?

BENTLEY

It's a pretty soft cop. The money's good. Plenty of super.

RICHARD

Always one jump ahead, weren't you?

BENTLEY

Well, I always like to be able to be in a position where I can cope with any given exigency at any given time.

(SANDY *looks at him.*)

RICHARD

That's the stuff.

BENTLEY

Well, anyway, it's good to get together again.

RICHARD

Yeah.

(*Pause.*)

BENTLEY

Say, how did you know where to find me?

RICHARD

Davo told me.

BENTLEY

Old Davo, eh?

RICHARD

Yes. He said you were expecting Simmo this afternoon. He said Simmo was a frequent visitor here.

SANDY

That's right.

RICHARD

Good friends with Simmo, are you Bentley?

SANDY

I am.

RICHARD

(*to* BENTLEY) Say, uh, I don't suppose you could have a word to Simmo and ask him if he could perhaps ... float me a bit of a loan, could you?

(*Pause.*)

BENTLEY

Would you like a beer?

RICHARD

Thanks.

(BENTLEY *goes out through the passageway.* SANDY *continues with her nails.* RICHARD *looks at her. Pause.*)

DIANE

Isn't this a beautiful place?

RICHARD

It certainly is.

SANDY

Yes, everyone raves about the unit.

RICHARD

So you're married to Bentley, eh?

SANDY

That's the present arrangement.

RICHARD

Funny to see old Bentley married. He was always a bit scared of girls. Never seemed to have the knack of cracking on. I remember he was wrapped in a bird called Doreen once, but he never made a move. Said he was biding his time, waiting for the right moment. But then Simmo got to her and it was too late. Old Bentley's got married, eh? I can hardly believe it.

SANDY

Neither can I.

RICHARD

Funny to see old Bentley married.

SANDY

What do you mean, 'funny'? What's so funny about it?

RICHARD

Well ... it's ... funny ...

SANDY

Do you mean funny ha ha or funny peculiar?

(*Pause.*)

RICHARD

Ha ha.

SANDY

Anyway, I won't be here for long. I'm on with Simmo now. We're going to make it together.

DIANE

I beg your pardon?

SANDY

I said Simmo and I are going to make it together.

DIANE

(*laughing*) Really, the fantasies some of these little hausfraus have!

SANDY

I'm Simmo's number one girl. We're going out this afternoon. He'll be here any minute.

DIANE

She must be dreaming. Simmo? Her? She's round the bend.

RICHARD

What's it to you, eh? What's it to you?

DIANE

Nothing.

RICHARD

(*to* SANDY) Could you sort of ... put in a good word to Simmo about me?

(*Pause.* BENTLEY *enters, carrying a tray on which there are four glasses of beer and a bottle.*)

BENTLEY

Here we are. The old Resch's. Just like old times, eh Richard?

(BENTLEY *hands the drinks around.* DIANE *sits down.*)

RICHARD

Yeah.

BENTLEY

Well, chug-a-lug.

RICHARD

Chug-a-lug.

SANDY

Chug-a-lug.

(*They look at her, hesitate, then drink.*)

RICHARD

Been playing tennis, have you?

BENTLEY

Yeah. We won the doubles cup today. We were down

two sets to love, then Gary got his big serve working, I chipped in at the net, and we were laughing. Towelled them up in no time.

SANDY

Congratulations.

(*Pause.* RICHARD *looks around.*)

RICHARD

Nice place you got here.

BENTLEY

Yes, it is rather. We've just moved in.

RICHARD

That's a very nice stereo set you've got there.

BENTLEY

A beauty, isn't it? Look what else I've got. (*He holds up the transistor radio.*)

RICHARD

What is it?

BENTLEY

A transistor radio, the latest model. Japanese.

RICHARD

Very compact, isn't it?

BENTLEY

Yes, it fits neatly into your pocket or purse. Pocket if you're a guy, and purse if you're a gal.

SANDY

Jesus.

(*Pause.*)

BENTLEY

Seen any of the old mob lately?

RICHARD

No, I seem to have lost touch.

BENTLEY

Yes, that tends to happen. You do lose touch.

RICHARD

Tell you what, I hear Hammo's back in town.

BENTLEY

Old chunder-guts, eh? He was a character, wasn't he?

RICHARD

A real character.

BENTLEY

We had some great times with old Hammo.

RICHARD

I'll say.

BENTLEY

Hey, do you remember the time he got pissed out of his mind and fronted up to this old duck and asked her for a root? It was Davo's mother! Jees I had to laugh. Nearly went off my face. Then the coppers came round and took him away. They put him in the paddy wagon with all the pros and cons. We had to go up to the cop shop and bail him out.

RICHARD

Bloody Hammo.

BENTLEY

He was a character, wasn't he?

RICHARD

A real character.

(*The women are looking rather bored.*)

BENTLEY

Remember the time he got sick at Davo's twenty-first and went for the big spit? He said to me, 'Jees I feel crook,' and then he raced across the room, shoved his head out the window and burped a rainbow. It went all over Davo and his bird in the bushes. What a mess!

SANDY

Jees I had to laugh. Nearly went off my face.

(*Pause.*)

BENTLEY

I didn't know you knew Hammo.

SANDY

I don't.

BENTLEY

But how—

SANDY

Skip it.

(*Pause.*)

RICHARD

Those were the days.

BENTLEY

Remember the time ...

(SANDY *gets up and storms out of the room, through the passageway.* BENTLEY *watches her, then continues, glancing over his shoulder a couple of times.*)

... when Hammo had a prang in his B and got dobbed in for neg driving?

RICHARD

Can't say I do.

BENTLEY

Well, Hammo had been on the grog and he didn't give way to his right and this bloke smashed into him. The bloke got all excited and was running all round the place like a mad thing, saying it was Hammo's fault. Well ...

(SANDY *enters, carrying a small step-ladder, which she places by the wall, L. They watch her. She goes out.* BENTLEY *continues uneasily.*)

Well, Hammo wouldn't have a bar of that. 'My fault?' he said. 'That's a laugh. It's a wonder you haven't got a defect notice for that old bomb of yours.' Well, the bloke took exception to that, as you can well imagine. Then he tried to job Hammo. Well, Hammo got stuck into him, I can tell you. Laid him out like a used frog. But then the ...

(SANDY *enters, carrying a hammer, nail, and a picture, a vivid red abstract.*)

Well, as I was saying, Hammo floored this twit, but then the coppers arrived and tried to pinch him ...

(SANDY *has climbed the ladder, and starts banging in the nail.* BENTLEY *tries to speak above the noise.*)

... but Hammo said—

RICHARD

What?

BENTLEY

(*louder*) Hammo said—

RICHARD

I can't hear you!

BENTLEY

(*shouting*) SANDY!!

(SANDY *stops hammering.*)

SANDY

What?

BENTLEY

Uh, now darling, we have guests here and I'm finding it a little difficult trying to converse with them while you're making such a noise.

SANDY

Oh.

BENTLEY

So if you could just postpone your domestic activities until a more appropriate time, we would be very grateful.

SANDY

(*coming down the ladder*) Well now, how could I refuse a request like that.

BENTLEY

Thank you, darling. That's most considerate of you.

SANDY

Don't mention it, darling. I only want to please you.

(BENTLEY *smiles and turns to* RICHARD.)

BENTLEY

Isn't she a sweetie? A real darling. Don't you think I've made a good catch, eh Richard?

(BENTLEY *tries to put his arm around* SANDY.)

SANDY

Back.

(BENTLEY *retreats.*)

BENTLEY

Well, uh, as I was saying, the coppers threw the book at Hammo and they—

SANDY

Would you like another beer, Richard? I see you've finished.

RICHARD

Uh, yes, thank you.

(SANDY *gets the bottle.*)

BENTLEY

But Hammo said that no mug copper ...

(SANDY *fills* RICHARD's *glass as* BENTLEY *speaks.*)

... is going to ... push me around ... but in the end they ... pinched him. Anyway, that's what happened when Hammo had a prang in his B.

(SANDY *sits down.*)

RICHARD

Bloody Hammo.

(SANDY *looks up at* RICHARD.)

SANDY

What do you do?

RICHARD

What do you mean?

SANDY

What do you do? For a living. Do you make a living?

DIANE

Richard's the editor of *The Inevitable Tarantula.*

SANDY

What's *The Inevitable Tarantula*?

DIANE

You mean to say you've never heard of *The Inevitable Tarantula*?

SANDY

That's right. I've never heard of it.

DIANE

Well! Some people just don't know what's happening.

RICHARD

It's a sort of magazine. An underground magazine for artists.

BENTLEY

Richard was always the arty one at school. Did cartoons ...

(SANDY *is looking at him*)

... humorous ...

SANDY

What else do you do?

RICHARD

I'm diversifying my activities in a number of different fields, like industrial design. I'm a painter mainly, but I do a few designs for the large glossies, too.

DIANE

You should have seen Richard's last one. It was a beaut design, a sort of tactile nightmare. He did this incredible white obelisk anchored into a beaut welter of blue streaks on a sheet of black strips with this incredible screen of pink flecks on a beaut steely surface.

SANDY

Sounds beaut.

DIANE

Richard's very clever, and he's got some very clever friends in the underground, too. It's marvellous fun. You meet all sorts of super people. Richard took me to a turn and I was really wrapped. There were all these incredibly tactile people throwing down Red Ned and saying such beaut things. Richard's got some fabulous friends. It's marvellous fun.

SANDY

Really?

DIANE

Richard's terribly clever. He's got tremendous artistic acumen and he's also abreast of the latest developments in industrial design.

BENTLEY

Yes, there has been a lot of astounding progress in industrial development in some of the many facets of modern technology.

(*Pause.* SANDY *stares at* BENTLEY *incredulously.*)

RICHARD

Bloody oath.

(RICHARD *sips his drink and looks at* SANDY.)

RICHARD

What do you do?

SANDY

Oh, lots of things. I'm always on the move, it's a mad whirl. I did a bit of modelling in Adelaide last year. And I'm thinking of doing a film in Melbourne in a month or two if I land a good role. I made a TV commercial here in Sydney not long ago.

RICHARD

What did you advertise?

SANDY

My legs.

(*Pause.*)

RICHARD

Oh.

(*He sips his drink.*)

SANDY

Panty-hose.

RICHARD

Oh, I see. That explains why ... your legs ...

SANDY

I found it a very absorbing experience.

RICHARD

Yes, I suppose it would be absorbing.

SANDY

I was absorbed, anyway.

RICHARD

What exactly did you have to do?

SANDY

Well, it started off with a B pulling up. It pulled up at the side of the street. I was driving it. I parked the car. Then the camera moved around and caught me getting out. I got out like this.

(*She moves her legs around to the side of the chair.*)

The camera was trained on my legs. I got out of the B.

(*She mimes it, and the rest of her speech.*)

I closed the door. Then I looked up and down the street. There was a man on the pavement.

(*She looks at* RICHARD.)

He looked at me. Then I went round to the parking meter. I stopped by the parking meter. The man was still watching me, but I didn't seem to mind. I gave the impression that I rather liked it. Then I slipped a coin in the slot of the meter. I walked across the pavement to a big glass building. I put my foot on the step like this. The camera was trained on my legs. The man's eyes followed me. I seemed to sense this, so I paused and looked around at him. He looked at me. Then I took a cigarette out of my bag and went up to him.

(*She takes a cigarette out of her bag and goes up to* RICHARD, *holding the cigarette out.*)

I asked him for a light.

(RICHARD *fumbles in his pocket and brings out a cigarette lighter. He flicks it on and a great sheet of flame, about ten inches high, shoots up. He hastily flicks it off, smiles weakly at* SANDY, *and adjusts the dial on the lighter. He flicks it on. A small flame hums.* SANDY *lights her cigarette from the flame. She looks at* RICHARD. *She is standing very close to him.*)

SANDY

Thank you.

(*Pause.*)

BENTLEY

Yes, and then what happened?

SANDY

(*impatiently*) Oh, then the jingle started—something about 'sheer ecstasy in Ecstasy Sheers.'

BENTLEY

Oh I get it. Sheer in both senses. And ecstasy—

SANDY

Yes!

(*She sits down. Pause.*)

RICHARD

Do you like working in the pubic service, Bentley?

(*Pause.* RICHARD *blushes slightly.* BENTLEY *considers the question.*)

BENTLEY

I can't supply you with an unqualified categorical 'yes' or 'no' answer to that particular question. However, I should like to make it abundantly clear that I consider the position eminently suitable on a number of counts, but equally unsuitable on a number of other counts.

(*Silence.*)

SANDY

(*a soft wail*) Christ.

(*Pause.*)

DIANE

I've never seen her in a TV commercial.

RICHARD

Haven't you?

DIANE

No. I don't believe a word she says.

(*The telephone rings.* SANDY *jumps up.*)

SANDY

That'll be Simmo.

(*She rushes over to the phone and picks up the receiver.*)

Hello? Who? Oh, no! Look, I've had enough of you. Just stop bothering me, see? You what? You want to what? Good God! Look, if you don't stop all this I'll get Simmo on to you, see?

(*She slams the receiver down.*)

BENTLEY

Anyone we know?

SANDY

It was that dreadful Davo. Never gives up, the big oaf. I wish he'd stop bothering me.

BENTLEY

I'll have to speak to him.

(SANDY *stares at* BENTLEY.)

SANDY

You'll have to what?

BENTLEY

I'll have a quiet word with him. You know intimate to him that you're not ... desirous ... to entertain his overtures.

SANDY

You mullet!

(*She sits down.*)

Do tell me a bit about yourself, Richard. What do you paint?

RICHARD

Pictures.

SANDY

I had already divined that. I mean, what sort? Abstract? Contemporary?

RICHARD

Well, contemporary, of course. I mean, we're all contemporary, aren't we? We're all alive.

SANDY

That's a moot point. Do you live at Paddington?

RICHARD

No.

SANDY

Oh. I would have thought you'd live at Paddington. And tell me, how long have you known the boy wonder?

RICHARD

Who?

SANDY

That. That over there. Whatsisname.

(BENTLEY *looks behind him.*)

RICHARD

That's Bentley. Your husband.

SANDY

I know.

RICHARD

You want to know how long I've known Bentley?

SANDY

Yes.

RICHARD

Oh. I didn't quite ... sort of ... understand ... to whom ... in effect ...

SANDY

Get on with it.

RICHARD

Yes well I've known Bentley since we were in kindergarten. We went through school, you see. We used to wag it together.

SANDY

Wag what?

RICHARD

Uh, school. Hookey, you know?

BENTLEY

Playing truant, I believe, is the correct expression for that particular misdemeanour.

SANDY

Thank you.

RICHARD

Well, anyway, Bentley and I lost touch after a while and this is the first time I've seen him for some years.

BENTLEY

Yes, it has been quite a while. You do lose touch.

RICHARD

How long have you two been married?

SANDY

A long, long time. I was quite young, what they call a slip of a girl, when Mr. Right turned up. That's him over there, in the neutral corner.

BENTLEY

I met Sandy at the local pictures one Saturday. It was a hot summer's night in the back stalls at the Roxy, and the organ was playing *Tea For Two*, and we were all eating Fantales and Sandy came in wearing a pink shift and I—

(*A car horn is heard.* SANDY *jumps up.*)

SANDY

At last! Simmo!

(*She rushes over to the sideboard to get her handbag.*)

Well, I'm off. Have yourselves a ball, peoples. There's a cold roast in the oven and a bottle of scotch in the cabinet so you should be set for the night. Ta-ta.

(*Meanwhile,* BENTLEY *has taken something quietly from the cabinet drawer. He holds it behind his back.*)

BENTLEY

Just a minute, Sandy.

(SANDY *has her hand on the door knob. She turns and looks at him.*)

I've got something for you.

(*Pause.*)

SANDY

What?

(*Pause.*)

BENTLEY

It's a surprise.

(*Pause.*)

SANDY

Well, what is it?

(*Pause.*)

BENTLEY

See if you can guess.

(*Silence.* BENTLEY *produces a package wrapped in gaily-coloured paper.*)

Happy birthday, darling.

(*Pause.*)

You thought I'd forgotten, didn't you?

(*He advances towards her, singing.*)

Happy birthday to you
Happy birthday to you
Happy birthday, dear—

(*He holds out the present to her. She knocks it to the floor, then goes out, slamming the door.* BENTLEY *looks at the closed door.*)

Happy ... birthday ... to ...

(DIANE *gets up.*)

DIANE

Would you excuse me for a moment, please.

RICHARD

Where are you going?

DIANE

I just want to see Simmo. I won't be a minute.

RICHARD

But he's going out with Sandy. I mean, uh, apparently.

DIANE

I won't be a minute.

(DIANE *goes out the front door.*)

BENTLEY

Well, that's the little woman.

RICHARD

She's quite a girl.

BENTLEY

Ar, she's a good kid.

(*Pause.*)

I love her very much.

(*Pause.*)

I think there's something troubling her. She hasn't been very happy lately. It's been a big worry to me.

(*Pause.*)

I'd like her to be happy.

(RICHARD *lights a cigarette.* BENTLEY *picks up the present and looks at it.*)

I bought her some panty-hose. Black mesh. They'll suit her.

(*Pause.*)

She's got lovely legs, don't you think?

(RICHARD *splutters on his cigarette.*)

RICHARD

Oh yes, lovely, lovely.

BENTLEY

She's a wonderful girl. I've always been very proud of her.

(*He looks at the present.*)

Black mesh.

RICHARD

I'm sure she'll like them.

(*Pause.*)

BENTLEY

Yes, I think there's something troubling her. I haven't heard her laugh for a long while. She used to be laughing all the time. Very gay. Always looked on the bright side of things. Very much alive. We used to go down to the beach. Park the B, dump the gear, and run into the surf, hand in hand. She'd hop about and shriek with joy. Pure joy. Like a child. Jumped up and down in the surf and splashed foam all over me. Not any more, though.

(*He puts the present back in the drawer.*)

Black mesh. I hope she likes them. She's a wonderful girl, don't you think?

RICHARD

Oh yes, wonderful. You're a very lucky man, Bentley.

BENTLEY

Yes, I've always been lucky.

(*Pause.*)

I won a chook at a pub once.

(*Pause.*)

Ay tell me, Richard, what exactly sort of made you come and see me after all this time?

(DIANE *comes in the front door.*)

RICHARD

What happened?

DIANE

Never mind.

BENTLEY

What made you come, Richard?

RICHARD

I wanted to see my old mate Bentley. I just thought we'd drop in, have a chat, sink a few ... you know?

BENTLEY

Yeah?

RICHARD

Of course.

BENTLEY

Well, on behalf of my wife and I, I'd like to extend to you the very warmest of welcomes.

(*Pause.*)

RICHARD

Thank you. Nice place you got here.

BENTLEY

Yes, everyone raves about the unit.

RICHARD

I'm very impressed with your stereo set.

BENTLEY

Beauty, isn't it?

RICHARD

I'll say. What sort of records you got?

BENTLEY

We have a large and comprehensive selection of the best recordings in the popular, classical, and evergreen categories.

(*Pause.*)

RICHARD

Great.

BENTLEY

Look what else I've got. A tape recorder. Little beauty, isn't it?

RICHARD

Yeah.

BENTLEY

I'll show you how it works.

(BENTLEY *switches on the machine, picks up the microphone and speaks into it.*)

Testing 1-2-3.

(*He reverses the tape to playback.* SANDY'S *voice is heard on the tape.*)

SANDY'S VOICE

I'm having it off with Simmo.

(BENTLEY'S *jaw drops. He turns off the tape recorder. He is very disconcerted. Silence.*)

DIANE

I think we'd better be going.

RICHARD

Yes, we must be off.

BENTLEY

Sure you won't stay and have another beer?

RICHARD

No thanks.

BENTLEY

Would you prefer a scotch?

RICHARD

No thanks. I like scotch, but not after beer.

DIANE

I like gin and tonic, but not after rum and coke.

RICHARD

Vodka's not bad, but it hits you hard afterwards.

BENTLEY

You can't drink on an empty stomach.

RICHARD

Once you mix your drinks you've had it.

BENTLEY

Ever had a middy of Bacardi neat?

RICHARD

Bond Seven and water's good for a hangover.

BENTLEY

Those Bloody Marys pack a punch.

RICHARD

I like a highball for a nightcap.

BENTLEY

I'll never forget the first time I sank a screwdriver.

RICHARD

I like a scotch after a beer.

(*Pause.*)

DIANE

We really must be going.

RICHARD

You'll be all right, Bentley.

BENTLEY

Would you like to stay and hear a record?

RICHARD

No thanks, we've got to go.

BENTLEY

All right.

RICHARD

You'll be right, mate. Buck up.

BENTLEY

I'm all right.

RICHARD

Don't worry about it, mate. She'll come back to you.

DIANE

She won't last long with Simmo.

RICHARD

You'll win her back.

BENTLEY

You think so?

RICHARD

Of course. Just assert yourself a bit. Throw your weight around. Be more aggressive.

DIANE

Yes, don't take it lying down.

RICHARD

Pull your socks up and have a bash.

DIANE

You've got nothing to lose.

RICHARD

You'll soon be out of this bad patch you're going through, so cheer up. You may be down, but you're not out. I mean, after all, when you come down to it, your predicament isn't exactly one of cosmic proportions, now is it?

DIANE

You just tripped over and fell on the floor.

RICHARD

Chin up and toe the line, you'll soon be back on your feet.

BENTLEY

I'll do that.

RICHARD

Take designing, for instance. In designing, it's a question

of putting things into context.

DIANE

It's the old relativity syndrome.

RICHARD

You've got to have a point of reference. It's the same with life.

DIANE

You've just got to have a point of reference.

RICHARD

It's as simple as that.

BENTLEY

I haven't got a point of reference.

RICHARD

Well, you see, then, that's where you're up yourself, isn't it? That's your trouble.

DIANE

You don't know whether you're slumming or growing.

RICHARD

You see, it's essential to have a framework to move in.

DIANE

Have you got a framework?

BENTLEY

No.

RICHARD

Well, that's your trouble, then, isn't it?

DIANE

You're between the deep blue sea and the frying pan.

RICHARD

You see, what you're lacking is an inner directive.

DIANE

You haven't got an inner directive.

RICHARD

That's your trouble.

DIANE

Too many put-on hang-ups, that's your problem.

RICHARD

What you really need is a meaningful stance.

BENTLEY

I haven't got a meaningful stance.

RICHARD

Well, you're buggered, then, aren't you? You've got to take action, get off your backside, move around. Think! Do! Be! Act!

(*Pause.*)

BENTLEY

Righto.

RICHARD

You've got no charisma.

DIANE

You've got a complex.

RICHARD

You need a rest.

DIANE

A complete break.

RICHARD

Rejuvenation.

DIANE

Regeneration.

RICHARD

Wake up to yourself.

DIANE

Wake up and live.

RICHARD

You'll be all right.

DIANE

You see what we mean?

BENTLEY

Yes.

RICHARD

Take the bull by the horns.

DIANE

Grab the nettle.

RICHARD

Face the facts.

DIANE

You'll be all right.

BENTLEY

Yes, I'll be all right. I'll take action.

RICHARD

That's the stuff. You'll win her back.

DIANE

Well, we'd better be going.

RICHARD

Yes, we really must fly. See you later, Bentley.

BENTLEY

Thanks for the advice.

DIANE

Think nothing of it.

RICHARD

It was a pleasure. After all, what are friends for?

DIANE

Goodbye.

BENTLEY

I could run you back in the B if you like.

RICHARD

No thanks, don't bother.

BENTLEY

Drop in any time. You know where we are.

RICHARD

Yes, it's a very easy place to find. You don't see many white hedges around these days.

BENTLEY

No, you don't.

RICHARD

Well, see you.

BENTLEY

Goodbye.

(RICHARD *opens the door.*)

Oh, Richard.

RICHARD

What?

BENTLEY

Don't do anything I wouldn't do.

(*Pause.*)

RICHARD

Goodbye Bentley.

BENTLEY

Goodbye Richard.

(RICHARD *and* DIANE *exit.* BENTLEY *sits down and puts his hands to his face. Silence. The tape recorder suddenly crackles to life and* BENTLEY'S *voice is heard on the tape.*)

BENTLEY'S VOICE

Testing 1-2-3.

(BENTLEY *picks up a cushion from the chair and hurls it at the tape recorder.*)

BLACKOUT

SCENE FOUR

Sunday afternoon, one week later. Lights up on SANDY *sitting in an armchair wearing a white dress. She is reading the Sunday paper and the audience can't see her face. Silence for a while, then* BENTLEY *enters, also dressed in white. He carries a quoit stand and five quoits. He places the quoit stand at the front of the stage and then steps back a few paces. He aims carefully, then throws the first quoit. It misses. He steadies himself and then throws the next four quoits very slowly, aiming carefully before each throw. They all miss and fall on the floor around the stand.* BENTLEY *stands very still and looks at the quoits on the floor. Then he looks at* SANDY, *who is still reading. Silence.* BENTLEY *goes over to the window and looks out of it. He lights a cigarette and gazes out of the window.* SANDY *continues reading.* BENTLEY *draws on his cigarette.*

CURTAIN

ACT TWO

SCENE ONE

The next day, Monday 6 p.m. Lights up on an empty stage. SANDY *comes in through the passageway, carrying the step ladder and the red abstract. She hangs it on the wall and then takes the step ladder out through the passageway. She re-enters and goes into the bedroom.* BENTLEY *comes in the front door, wearing a suit and carrying a briefcase, a box of chocolates and a large bunch of flowers. He puts down the briefcase and holds the chocolates and flowers behind his back.*

BENTLEY

Sandy? Where are you?

(*Pause.*)

Sandy?

(SANDY *comes out of the bedroom carrying a suitcase. She puts it down by the front door and goes back into the bedroom. She is wearing a black cocktail dress.*)

What's this? What are you doing with my suitcase?

(SANDY *comes out of the bedroom carrying an airways bag.*)

What's the idea? What are you doing?

(SANDY *puts the bag down by the front door and goes back into the bedroom. Small pieces of* BENTLEY's *gear—clothes, towels, tennis racquet, etc., are flung out through the bedroom door.* BENTLEY *goes over to the door.*)

I demand an explanation. I demand that you stop this immediately.

(BENTLEY *ducks and a basketball bounces out over his head.* SANDY *comes out of the bedroom brushing her hair.*)

SANDY

Simmo's moving in.

BENTLEY

What?

SANDY

You're moving out.

BENTLEY

Moving out? Moving out of my unit? You've got to be joking.

(*Pause.* SANDY *continues brushing her hair.*)

You are joking, aren't you?

(*Pause.*)

In here? In my unit? I won't allow it.

(*Pause.*)

Look, uh, I bought you some chocolates and flowers, darling.

(*Pause.*)

Maybe I haven't treated you too well lately, darling. I don't know.

(*Pause.*)

Look, I tell you what. Let's go out to dinner tonight. I'll give you the works—cocktails, dinner by candlelight at a good restaurant, then a show, coffee at the Cross, and home to bed. What do you say, huh?

SANDY

I'm going out to dinner with Simmo tonight.

BENTLEY

You could ring him up and say you've got a headache. Tell him a little white lie. Say you've got the pain you can't explain.

SANDY

You can move out now or you can sleep out here tonight and find a flat tomorrow.

BENTLEY

That's ridiculous. I'm your husband.

SANDY

I know.

BENTLEY

You can't just throw me out.

SANDY

Why not?

(*Pause.*)

BENTLEY

Would you like to put these flowers in a vase?

(*Pause.* BENTLEY *reaches into his briefcase and brings out a copy of the* Ladies' Home Journal.)

I, uh, I've been doing a bit of reading, darling. I read this article in the *Ladies' Horne Journal* called 'Can This Marriage Be Saved?' I think it's pretty relevant to our problem, darling. Would you like to hear it?

(*Pause. He reads:*)

The trouble with Harry and Lottie's marriage was that they didn't share each other's interests. So the next vacation they sent Troy and Mary-Jane off to summer camp and went fishing together at one of Harry's favourite haunts.

(*Pause.*)

Would you like to come to the pub tomorrow night with me and Davo?

SANDY

You're moving out.

BENTLEY

What?

SANDY

Simmo's moving in.

BENTLEY

Over my dead body.

SANDY

If you insist.

(*Pause.*)

BENTLEY

You seem to have changed, darling. You seem all hard and cruel. You used to be a ... terrific bird. I'd never have got to grade three if it hadn't been for you. Behind every successful man ... you know? Alan White reckons I'm a moral for grade four, but I can't do it without you, darling.

(*Pause.*)

Remember the night we met? That night at the Roxy?

I fell down the stairs and you said I was so helpless I needed someone to look after me. Do you remember that, darling?

SANDY

Stop it, Bentley.

BENTLEY

Look, why don't we just kiss and make up, eh?

SANDY

No.

BENTLEY

Would you like to open the chocolates?

SANDY

No.

BENTLEY

You're not being very co-operative, darling.

(*Pause.*)

You can't be serious. How can Simmo possibly move in here? This is my unit. That's my stereo set. You're my wife. You're my lawful wedded wife. You can't have Simmo in here. It's illegal. I can't envisage it. Simmo in my unit? It's out of the question. It's not on the board. You can't be serious.

SANDY

Look, what are you going to do? Simmo's moving in. What are you going to do?

BENTLEY

Simmo's not moving in here.

SANDY

He's moving in tonight.

BENTLEY

You're not having him here. Not in our home unit. I won't allow it.

SANDY

Won't you?

BENTLEY

No. I mean, I've got nothing against Simmo. I like the guy. I've found him to be an agreeable companion on a number of occasions. But he's shown a complete disregard for common courtesy.

SANDY

Has he?

BENTLEY

Yes. Look, if he's putting the hard word on you, if he's being in any way coercive, if he's employing intimidatory tactics of any kind, I'll take care of it. I'll have a man to man chat with him. Off the cuff, straight from the shoulder, no punches pulled. Everything open and above board. Clear the air, you know? Simmo's a good bloke, I'm open to reason, we'll work it out. We'll solve the problem. We'll nut it out together, me and Simmo. It'll be all taken care of.

SANDY

Je-sus.

BENTLEY

Well, what do you say?

SANDY

Simmo is moving in. You are moving out. Do I make myself clear?

(*Pause.*)

BENTLEY

Yes, darling, you have expressed your sentiments with force and clarity. However, the fact remains that Simmo is not moving in here. I don't like to be disagreeable, darling, but I feel that this proposal cannot be entertained under any circumstances. I'm sorry, but I can't allow him in here and that's that. Now if you would be so kind as to restore my personal effects to their proper place, I would be most grateful.

SANDY

Taking a firm stand, are you?

BENTLEY

You bet I am.

SANDY

Won't you relent?

BENTLEY

Certainly not.

SANDY

Pretty please?

BENTLEY

No.

SANDY

Well, I guess that's that, then.

BENTLEY

I'm putting my foot down.

SANDY

Please, oh please change your mind. Won't you relent? Won't you show us a little mercy? Where's your charity? Please let Simmo in. Please let him stay here. Please don't hurt him. I beg of you.

BENTLEY

(*beaten*) I'm ... taking a ... firm stand.

(*A car horn is heard.*)

SANDY

There's Simmo now.

(BENTLEY *clears his throat hastily.*)

BENTLEY

On the other hand, taking into account the extenuating circumstances motivating this plaintive request, I feel duty bound to reconsider the matter in the light of subsequent events.

SANDY

Thanks. You can sleep out here till you find a flat, if you like, or you can move out right now. Anyway, clean this place up. I'm going out to dinner with Simmo and when we come back I want this place to look clean.

(SANDY *goes out the front door.* BENTLEY *stares after her. He looks around the room.*)

FADE OUT

SCENE TWO

The following day, Tuesday, 6 p.m. BENTLEY *sits in an armchair reading a newspaper.* SANDY *comes in wearing her black cocktail dress with lots of jewellery. She puts a tablecloth over the table and goes back out the passageway. She returns with expensive-looking china and cutlery and sets two places at the table. She puts out two wine glasses, an ice bucket with a bottle of champagne in it, and then brings out a candle-holder with one long candle in it. She lights the candle. During these preparations,* BENTLEY *keeps looking out from behind his newspaper. He tries to feign indifference.* SANDY *completes setting the table, and sits down in an armchair. She glances at her watch, brings out a small mirror from her handbag, and pats her hair into place.* BENTLEY *looks at her.*

FADE OUT

SCENE THREE

The following day, Wednesday, 10 p.m. Lights up on an empty stage. SANDY *can be heard giggling with pleasure from the bedroom, then silence.* BENTLEY *enters through the passageway, wearing pyjamas and bed socks and carrying a towel over his shoulder. He glances at the bedroom door, then gets into a makeshift bed, consisting of the two armchairs pushed together, with a rug over them. He reads the* Ladies' Home Journal. SANDY *giggles again.* BENTLEY *looks at the bedroom door, then returns to his reading.* SANDY *starts giggling continuously.* BENTLEY *tries to continue reading, but then puts the magazine down in front of him.* SANDY *stops giggling.* BENTLEY *goes over to the wall and takes down the red abstract. He looks through a peephole into the bedroom. Silence. He wanders away, deep in thought, then goes out purposefully through the passageway and returns, carrying a hose, with his finger over the nozzle. He puts the hose through the peephole, and holds it there. Then, after a few moments, he withdraws it cautiously. There is no water coming out of the hose. He puts the hose back in the peephole, runs out through the passageway, and returns. He holds the hose, then cautiously withdraws it from the peephole. No water comes out of the hose. He runs out through the passageway, returns and holds the hose. He withdraws it cautiously. No water comes out of it. He peers up the nozzle. The hose squirts water in his face, then stops. He throws the hose on the floor. He strides out through the passageway and comes back with an air rifle. He marches up to the bedroom door, flings it open, stands back and aims the air rifle. He moves the barrel up and down, rhythmically. He is about to shoot when there is a knock on the door.* BENTLEY *hesitates, then lowers the rifle, closes the bedroom door, goes over and opens the front door.* GARY *and* DIANE *come in.* GARY *holds a large trophy. They both wear jeans and T-shirts depicting surfing scenes on the front.*

BENTLEY

Gary?

GARY

Bentley.

BENTLEY

Gary.

GARY

Bentley.

BENTLEY

Hello Gary.

GARY

Hello Bentley.

(Pause.)

You know Diane, don't you?

BENTLEY

Hello Diane.

DIANE

Hello Bentley.

(Pause.)

BENTLEY

Well, good to see you.

GARY

Yeah. We just dropped in. Nothing special.

DIANE

We just dropped in.

BENTLEY

What have you been up to?

GARY

Nothing much. What about you?

BENTLEY

Ar, just mucking around as usual. *Comme ci, comme ça.* Been down the rubbity lately?

GARY

No, I haven't hit the hops for a couple of weeks. Why?

BENTLEY

Nothing. You haven't heard anything about me, have you? Any sort of ... rumours, have you?

GARY

Rumours?

BENTLEY

Yes.

GARY

No.

BENTLEY

That's good. You know how these things get around ... give a false impression ... just a pack of lies.

GARY

What sort of rumours?

BENTLEY

Oh, you know the kind of thing ... absolute rubbish. Smoke with no fire. So you haven't heard anything?

GARY

Not a word.

BENTLEY

That's great.

GARY

How's Sandy?

BENTLEY

Fine, just fine.

GARY

That's great. How's the world been treating you?

BENTLEY

No worries.

GARY

Glad to hear it.

BENTLEY

Well, how about a beer?

GARY

Wouldn't say no.

BENTLEY

Won't be a minute.

(BENTLEY *goes out through the passageway.*)

DIANE

Well, where is he?

GARY

Probably in the bedroom.

DIANE

With her?

GARY

Probably.

DIANE

What could he want with her?

GARY

A game of bridge, probably.

DIANE

I don't understand it. She's a nothing.

GARY

Look, what's it to you?

DIANE

Nothing.

GARY

Eh?

DIANE

Forget it.

GARY

You couldn't possibly be aspiring to Simmo's cot, now could you?

DIANE

Of course I'm not. What a suggestion!

GARY

It's just as well.

DIANE

Why?

GARY

I've seen it happen time and again. You stick with me.

DIANE

Of course I'll stick with you. What do you think I am?

(*Pause.*)

Of course I'll stick with you.

(BENTLEY *re-enters with three beers.*)

BENTLEY

Here we are. The old Resch's.

GARY

Thanks, mate.

BENTLEY

Chug-a-lug.

GARY

Chug-a-lug.

DIANE

Cheers. (*They drink.*)

BENTLEY

Just dropped in, have you?

GARY

Yes, we were passing by and we thought we might pop in and see our old mate Bentley.

DIANE

We saw Simmo's B outside.

BENTLEY

Oh?

DIANE

Yes. We thought we might pop in and see our old friend Simmo.

BENTLEY

Did you?

DIANE

Yes. Gary wants a job in Simmo's firm.

BENTLEY

What firm?

GARY

Simmo Enterprises Ltd.

BENTLEY

I'm sorry to disappoint you, but Simmo's not here.

DIANE

But we saw his B outside.

BENTLEY

You must have been mistaken.

DIANE

You can't mistake Simmo's B.

BENTLEY

The Prime Minister's got a flat on the ground floor. Maybe Simmo's visiting the Prime Minister.

(*Pause.*)

GARY

Where's Sandy?

BENTLEY

She's in bed. She was very tired.

(*Pause.*)

GARY

Nice place you've got here. Must be handy to the beach.

BENTLEY

Yes, hop in the B, you're there in a tick.

(GARY *picks up* BENTLEY'S *air rifle.*)

GARY

Say, is this your old air rifle?

BENTLEY

That's the one.

GARY

I remember you had this at school.

BENTLEY

Yeah. Remember the time we got every street light along the beach that night?

GARY

Do I ever! Remember that old duck who chased us up the promenade?

BENTLEY

She had Buckley's. Remember the time when Hammo knocked off the light in front of the cop shop?

GARY

Bloody Hammo. Hey, remember the time when you shot Simmo in the arse in the playground at school?

BENTLEY

Yes.

GARY

Hey, look, there's still a dent in the barrel where Simmo hit you on the head.

(*Pause.*)

BENTLEY

(*to* DIANE) Can I top up your glass?

DIANE

No thanks.

GARY

Reminds me of the time when Hammo told Simmo he didn't like the way Simmo was running the playground. Poor Hammo. He was in a coma for three days. Still, he was the only bloke who ever stood up to Simmo.

(*Pause.*)

BENTLEY

What's the trophy for?

DIANE

Gary won the Senior Surf Race at the Manly Surf Carnival.

BENTLEY

Congratulations.

DIANE

Isn't he marvellous?

GARY

Ar jees.

DIANE

We're going on a surfari next week. We're going up the coast in Gary's B. I love surfing. Gary lent me his board one day and I was really wrapped. It's the only thing worth doing. We're going to take three weeks off and follow the sun.

BENTLEY

Great.

DIANE

Gary's managed to successfully bridge the gap between the surf clubs and the board riders. He's both a club member and a board rider. He's been the first to bridge this great chasm.

(DIANE *puts the trophy down on the sideboard beside* BENTLEY'S *much smaller tennis trophy.*)

BENTLEY

It's a very handsome trophy.

GARY

Thanks.

DIANE

We're going to show it to Simmo.

BENTLEY

Why?

DIANE

It's Gary's reference. Simmo's bound to ask Gary to join his firm when he sees the trophy.

BENTLEY

What sort of firm is this Simmo Enterprises Ltd?

GARY

Well, it's sort of hard to explain, Bentley.

DIANE

It's very exciting.

BENTLEY

I see.

(SANDY *giggles from the bedroom.*)

GARY

What was that?

BENTLEY

What?

GARY

That noise.

BENTLEY

I didn't hear anyone giggling.

GARY

Maybe I was mistaken.

DIANE

Well, I think we'd better be going.

GARY

Sure you haven't seen Simmo?

BENTLEY

Positive.

DIANE

You don't know where we could find him?

BENTLEY

No idea. Try the pub.

GARY

Righto. Well, see you, Bentley.

BENTLEY

See you.

GARY

If you do happen to bump into Simmo, then—(SANDY *whirls out of the bedroom, wearing a short flimsy nightdress with a see-through top.*)

SANDY

Simmo wants a cigarette. Are there any cigarettes?

(*Pause.*)

I said Simmo wants a cigarette.

(*Pause.*)

What are you doing here?

GARY

We just dropped in.

DIANE

We were just passing by and we dropped in.

SANDY

Oh. Have you got any cigarettes? Simmo wants a cigarette.

GARY

Here you are.

(GARY *hands her a packet of cigarettes.*)

SANDY

Thank you.

GARY

Give my regards to Simmo.

(DIANE *walks over to the bedroom door.*)

SANDY

What do you think you're doing?

DIANE

Just having a look.

SANDY

How dare you snoop around in my unit!

GARY

Come on, Diane. Cut it out.

(DIANE *goes over to the armchair and sits down, guided by* GARY.)

SANDY

What's the matter with you? Is that how you get your kicks? Are you a voyeur? We've already had one voyeur this evening. A Peeping Tom. Looking at us. Getting an eyeful. How do you think we feel? Uh?

GARY

She's sorry.

SANDY

I mean, I'm liberal-minded, but I draw the line at voyeurs. So does Simmo. He'll take action if there's any more.

GARY

There won't be any more. Tell Simmo I've put a stop to it.

SANDY

I should think so. We don't like it. I mean, we've already got a resident Peeping Tom as it is. A full-time voyeur. We don't want any more. One's more than enough. Anyway, we're getting rid of him. He's going to leave. Isn't he?

(*Pause.*)

Isn't he?

(*Pause.*)

Yes, we're getting rid of him. I mean, it's a bit much, isn't it? Simmo finds it very tiresome. What do you suggest we do?

GARY

I'm ... not sure.

BENTLEY

Would anyone like another beer?

(*Pause.*)

SANDY

Bentley is a public servant. He's a very good public servant. They think very highly of him in the department. I'm very proud of Bentley. Very proud. I gave him five years of my nubile period. Five years.

BENTLEY

Five and a half.

SANDY

Five and a half. But all good things must come to an end, don't you feel? You can have too much of a good thing, don't you agree?

GARY

I'm ... not sure.

SANDY

You're not sure? I think it's very clear-cut. It's as plain as the nose on your little friend's face. It's crystal clear. There's only one course of action, don't you think? Uh?

GARY

I'm not ... certain.

SANDY

Well I am. I'm certain. Thanks for the cigarettes.

(*She goes back into the bedroom. Silence.*)

BENTLEY

That's a very nice trophy you've got there, Gary.

GARY

You like it?

BENTLEY

Very much.

GARY

Thanks.

DIANE

Nice place you've got here.

BENTLEY

You like it?

DIANE

Very much.

BENTLEY

Thanks.

(*Pause.* GARY *gets up. So does* DIANE.)

GARY

I think we'd better be going.

DIANE

It's getting late.

BENTLEY

Yes.

GARY

Thanks for the grog.

BENTLEY

My pleasure.

(*Pause.*)

GARY

Don't worry about it too much, Bentley. You'll be all right.

DIANE

Yes, don't let her upset you.

GARY

Just ignore her.

BENTLEY

I'll do that.

DIANE

Don't take any notice of her.

BENTLEY

I don't.

GARY

What you should do is get out and about more.

DIANE

There are plenty of other fish in the sea.

GARY

Find yourself another bird.

DIANE

That'll make her jealous.

GARY

Don't let it get you down.

DIANE

Live it up.

GARY

Have a bash.

DIANE

Take a chance.

GARY

Play it cool.

DIANE

What can you lose?

GARY

You'll be home and hosed in no time.

BENTLEY

You reckon?

GARY

Look, why don't you come down to the pub tomorrow night? Have a few beers, forget your worries. You might bump into Hammo down there.

BENTLEY

Hammo?

GARY

Yes, I hear he's back in town.

BENTLEY

Old Hammo, eh? I hope he makes it.

GARY

I'll line up a bird for you, too. I know a couple of grunters.

DIANE

You'll be all right.

GARY

What do you say?

BENTLEY

I'll see you tomorrow.

GARY

Great. Well, we'll be off.

DIANE

Goodbye.

GARY

Find your feet, get your head down, keep your eye on the ball.

DIANE

Keep your eyes peeled and your nose clean.

GARY

You've got to get your foot in the door before you throw your weight around. That's the first step. The second step is to put your best foot forward. And step number three is to keep on your toes. Follow me?

BENTLEY

Yes.

DIANE

Don't worry about it. Simmo won't be here for long.

GARY

See you tomorrow.

BENTLEY

Hoo roo.

GARY

Oh, by the way. Here are the photos from your house-warming party.

(GARY *hands some photos to* BENTLEY. BENTLEY *looks at them.*)

BENTLEY

Thanks.

GARY

There's a good snap of you and Sandy by the stereo set.

BENTLEY

Beauty.

GARY

See you.

(GARY *and* DIANE *go out the front door.* BENTLEY *sits doom and puts his hands to his face. Then he turns off the top light and reads in bed by the light of the lamp.* SANDY *comes quietly out of the bedroom. She looks at him.*)

SANDY

Are you awake, Bentley?

BENTLEY

Yes.

SANDY

What are you reading?

BENTLEY

The *Ladies' Home Journal.*

SANDY

Is it interesting?

BENTLEY

Oh yes. I'm reading about how Chuck and Betty's marriage was on the rocks because of in-law trouble.

SANDY

That's nice. Are you comfortable there?

BENTLEY

Oh yes. I was a bit stiff after the first night, but I put a cushion in the crook of my back and slept like a log.

SANDY

That's good. It must be a bit awkward, having to sleep out here.

BENTLEY

Well, like everything else, it has its virtues and its defects, but in the long run, taking into account all the relevant factors, the defects outweigh the virtues.

SANDY

Yes, I suppose they would.

BENTLEY

This doesn't mean that the virtues are non-existent. Far from it. It's just that they are disproportionate to the defects.

(BENTLEY *puts his fist into his mouth and bites it hard.*)

SANDY

Of course. Now, Bentley, Simmo and I have just had a small conference, and he was all for ... causing you bodily harm. He was going to inflict bodily pain on you. He felt that it was a necessary step to take, and one which was essential to his personal well-being. But I prevented him. I said: 'Bentley will go. You leave it to me.' So there you have it. Either you go, or ... well ...

BENTLEY

I don't see why I should go.

SANDY

You don't?

BENTLEY

No. It's my unit. I live here.

SANDY

I see.

BENTLEY

A man's home is his castle.

SANDY

Go on.

BENTLEY

That's a review of the current situation, from my point of view.

SANDY

That's your considered opinion, is it?

BENTLEY

Yes.

(*Pause.*)

SANDY

I think I've been very patient. I've been able to retain my cool. But really, I do think that you're taking me within sight of breaking point. I'm in control, I've maintained my equanimity, but I'm on the brink, do you understand? Are you going to play ball? Are you going to get out? Or is Simmo going to have to break your skull?

BENTLEY

I don't feel we've considered all the available alternatives.

SANDY

You see this air rifle? Would you like Simmo to wrap it round your head?

(*Pause.*)

Look, Simmo can't stand it any longer. There's been talk down at the pub. Adverse comment. He's had to thump three blokes in the last week. They were making jokes. How do you think I feel? I'll be a laughing stock if this keeps up. You'll have to go. There's no alternative. If you're not out by the end of the week, then ... (*shrugging*) huh ...

BENTLEY

I'll consider your request.

SANDY

Look, Benny ...

(*Pause. They look at each other.*)

Look, I don't want to see you get hurt. So just move out, will you?

(*Pause.*)

It's finished, Bentley. It's all over.

BENTLEY

Is it?

SANDY

Yes.

BENTLEY

I'm sorry, but I've worked very hard for this unit, and I'm the legal tenant of the premises, and I will not be forced out of my unit. I will not give up the ship. Anyone desirous of buying my property will have to submit their proposal through the proper channels.

SANDY

You'll be sorry.

(SANDY *goes back into the bedroom.* BENTLEY *lights a cigarette and smokes nervously. He goes to the telephone, dials a number, and waits.*)

BENTLEY

Hello? Could I speak to your sergeant, please constable? Yes, maybe you could. I have a complaint to make. Is it strictly legal for a bloke to break into another bloke's unit and kick out the bloke who owns the unit? That's what I thought. Yes, it's happened to me. Would you? Great. I'll see you in five minutes. Oh, uh, Simmo. Hello? Hello? Hello?

(*He hangs up. Then he dials another number.*)

Hello? Sorry to disturb you at this hour, Mr. Shapiro, but I've got a very urgent legal problem on my hands. Well, a bloke's moved into my unit and now he's going to kick me out. Yes. That's what I reckon. Good. Well, uh, Simmo. What do you mean, I haven't got a leg to stand on legally? Hello? Hello? Hello?

(BENTLEY *hangs up and goes back to bed. He stares in front of him, then picks up his magazine and reads.* SANDY *giggles from the bedroom.* BENTLEY *puts down the magazine and stares in front of him.* SANDY *giggles again.*)

SCENE FOUR

The following evening, 6 p.m. Lights up on an empty stage. BENTLEY *enters through the passageway, wearing jeans and a T-shirt. He picks up his suitcase and puts it by the front door. He switches on the tape recorder, picks up the microphone, and speaks into it.*

BENTLEY

Dear Sandy. This is your husband Bentley speaking. In view of recent events, and taking all the various factors appertaining to the situation into consideration, I wish to inform you that I am leaving you for a period of trial separation. Being married to you, while enjoyable in many aspects, has placed severe limitations on my freedom of movement, as I have what may be termed a roving eye, and wish to indulge my inclinations in that field of endeavour. I have decided to seek greater freedom and greener pastures and will embark on a new way of life. As I set out to seek my fortune, I leave you with a thought for today which I hope will console you: It is better to have loved and lost than never to have loved at all, so don't feel too badly about it. The same thing happened to Chuck and Betty when their marriage went on the rocks. So there it is. I'll say goodbye now, and embark on my new way of life, freed from all shackles, and eager to embrace new experiences. I don't wanna break your heart, woman, but hell, I gotta keep a-travellin' on. So it's time to say goodbye, I guess. This is your husband Bentley signing off. Goodnight and God bless.

(He switches off the machine, looking very pleased with himself. Then he switches to playback. SANDY'S *voice is heard on the tape.)*

SANDY'S VOICE

Piss off.

BLACKOUT

CURTAIN

ACT THREE

SCENE ONE

The following Saturday morning. The curtain rises on another curtain, a black one, a few feet behind it. Dangling on a string from the ceiling is a meat pie. It is about six feet off the floor. Silence for a while, then RICHARD *and* GARY *enter from opposite sides and walk up to the pie. They look at it.* GARY *carries a rifle. They look at the pie. Silence.*

GARY

Is this it?

RICHARD

That's it.

GARY

Is this all?

RICHARD

Yes.

(*Pause.*)

GARY

Very effective.

RICHARD

You like it?

GARY

Very much.

RICHARD

Thanks.

GARY

It's a beauty.

RICHARD

I'm happy with it.

GARY

What's it called?

RICHARD

'Still Life'.

GARY

Very appropriate.

RICHARD

You think so?

GARY

Very much so.

RICHARD

Thanks.

GARY

It's well named.

RICHARD

I'm glad to hear it.

(GARY *pushes the pie. It swings to and fro like a pendulum.*)

GARY

What do you call it now?

RICHARD

'Pie in the Sky'.

GARY

Very apt.

RICHARD

Do you think so?

GARY

I do indeed.

RICHARD

Thanks.

(*Pause.* GARY *looks around.*)

GARY

Bit stuffy in here.

(RICHARD *stops the pie swinging, then goes to the side of the stage and pulls the black curtain back, revealing the rest of the room.*)

That's better.

RICHARD

I always like to keep the still lifes separated when they're being shown for the first time.

GARY

Good idea.

(*They walk back into the main part of* RICHARD's *room. It is designed the same way as* BENTLEY's *living room, with a door, down R., a passageway up L., and a window in the right wall, upstage. The walls are brown. There are paintings everywhere and a junk sculpture in a prominent position. It consists of an old cash register with two giant pink plastic handles, mounted on a stand. There is a bed, bookcase, chairs, tables, record-player, and a curved Japanese sword mounted on the back hall.)*

Mum tells me you're leaving us.

(RICHARD *starts packing a suitcase and tidying up the room.)*

RICHARD

That's right. I've decided to go bush and sort myself out.

GARY

What happened to that magazine you edited?

RICHARD

Unfortunately *The Inevitable Tarantula* is now defunct. I tried to borrow some money to keep it afloat, but I failed. Then all my staff walked out on me, including my old friend Diane.

GARY

She's a tart, that one.

RICHARD

She's a whore.

GARY

Well, she's finally got what she wants.

RICHARD

Yes. So there you are. I dropped the lot. I battled away on the outer for years, but where did it get me? I'm going bush, mate. They can all get stuffed.

GARY

Anyway, Richard, we'll be sorry to lose you. You've been a model tenant.

RICHARD

I do my best.

GARY

Bet you'll miss Mum's cooking.

RICHARD

Yes.

GARY

No more rissoles for breakfast.

RICHARD

No.

GARY

Well, I suppose I'd better be off.

RICHARD

Going hunting, are you?

GARY

Yeah, going up to Werris Creek for the weekend.

RICHARD

Who with?

GARY

Simmo, of course. He'll be round any minute to pick me up in the B. He knows all the best places to go.

RICHARD

Well, have a good time.

GARY

We will, mate, don't worry. We always do. Gaw, I remember the last time we went up the country with Simmo. Did I ever tell you about it? We had a great time. We blew into this little hick town on a Saturday morning and by midnight that night do you know what Simmo had done?

RICHARD

No, Gary, do tell me.

GARY

He backed five winners at the picnic races, floored three locals in a brawl, demolished a niner, and torpedoed the minister's daughter. Anglican, she was. High Church.

RICHARD

Bloody Simmo, eh?

GARY

I bet they're still talking about it. But you wait till we hit Werris Creek tonight, mate, it'll be even wilder. Gaw, I remember the last time we were there. We had a great time that day. I was in the pub having a quiet beer with a few Werris Creek identities, when this bloke came up and started picking a blue with Simmo. Christ! It was suicide! Well, anyway, he copped the lot from Simmo, as you can well imagine. I couldn't bear to watch it, so I ducked out for a Johnny Bliss. But when I came back it was a real donnybrook—Simmo took on the lot of them and came out without a scratch.

RICHARD

That's Simmo for you.

GARY

Bloody oath. What a man!

RICHARD

What a man.

GARY

Anyway, Richard, I'll be off now. All the best.

RICHARD

Same to you.

GARY

Keep on with your art, mate. You'll crack it one day, I'm sure of it. I mean, you're nobody's fool, mate. You've got a bit of nouse.

RICHARD

Thanks, Gary.

GARY

I mean, you might be an arty sort of bloke, but you've got your head screwed on the right way. You don't bung on the bull like a lot of these blokes you see around the place these days. Now take these pictures, for instance. Now I wouldn't pretend to know what they're all about, because maybe I'm not too cluey about this sort of thing. But I do know this: you're not bunging on the bull, mate.

RICHARD

Thanks, Gary, I try to keep it clean. As a matter of fact, I remember when I had my one and only exhibition at an art gallery, there was a whole lot of scientists there, bunging it on. They were on a lunch-break from a convention on dynamics and they said my work was symptomatic.

GARY

Symptomatic, eh?

RICHARD

Yes.

GARY

They were having you on.

RICHARD

That occurred to me, Gary.

GARY

What a lot of bull-artists. Bloody scientists. What were they doing in an art gallery, anyway? But you're not like that, Richard. You're a good bloke. You play it straight.

RICHARD

Thank you, Gary.

GARY

Well, I must say it's been a pleasure having you here, Richard. You've done the right thing by me and I'd say I've done the right thing by you, and you can't do better than that. I mean, if a bloke, no matter who he is, does the right thing by a bloke, and that bloke does the right thing by the other bloke, then you can't go fairer than that, now can you?

RICHARD

I don't think so.

GARY

Anyway, take care of yourself, don't get on the hops too much, keep your nose clean and your feet dry and you can't go wrong.

RICHARD

I'll do that, Gary.

GARY

All the best, mate.

RICHARD

Same to you.

GARY

Drop us a line.

RICHARD

Will do.

GARY

Take care.

RICHARD

Keep in touch.

GARY

Will do.

(*There is a knock on the door.*)

RICHARD

Come in.

(BENTLEY *enters timidly. He wears jeans and a T-shirt and carries a suitcase.*)

Bentley?

BENTLEY

Gary?

RICHARD

Hello Bentley.

BENTLEY

Hello Richard, Gary.

GARY

Bentley.

(*Pause.*)

RICHARD

Well, this is a surprise.

BENTLEY

Yes.

GARY

What brings you here, Bentley?

BENTLEY

I just thought I'd drop in on my old mates.

RICHARD

Good to see you.

BENTLEY

I don't suppose you've seen Hammo around, have you?

RICHARD

Not recently.

GARY

I hear he's back in town.

BENTLEY

Good. I hope I can find him.

(GARY *looks at his watch and goes to the window.*)

GARY

Simmo should be here any minute.

BENTLEY

Who?

GARY

Simmo.

BENTLEY

Oh.

RICHARD

Gary's going shooting with Simmo.

BENTLEY

That's nice.

GARY

How are things with you, Bentley?

BENTLEY

Fine. Just fine.

RICHARD

How's the old public service?

BENTLEY

I don't know. I tossed it in.

GARY

What?

RICHARD

Well, who'd have thought!

BENTLEY

Yeah, does seem a bit strange. No more super.

GARY

Why'd you leave?

(BENTLEY *clears his throat.*)

BENTLEY

I decided I needed to undergo some reorientation of the underlying factors governing my basic attitudes to life, liberty, and the pursuit of happiness.

(*Pause.*)

RICHARD

Good idea.

BENTLEY

Anyway, I was about to get the boot from work, so I decided to resign. Simmo rang up my department. Had a word to Alan White and out I went.

GARY

Bad luck.

BENTLEY

Not really. I was sick of the place. I was in a rut, you see. I felt that life has more to offer.

RICHARD

You reckon?

GARY

(*looking out the window*) Here's Simmo now.

(*A car horn is heard.* BENTLEY *dives under* RICHARD's *bed.*)

What on earth ...?

RICHARD

Hey Bentley! What's going on?

GARY

It was only a car horn.

RICHARD

What's the matter, Bentley? Come out of there. What are you scared of?

GARY

Maybe he's scared of Simmo.

BENTLEY

Scared of Simmo? That's a laugh. Ha!

RICHARD

Come out from under that bed. You're making a fool of yourself.

BENTLEY

Who says I'm scared of Simmo? I could take him any day.

GARY

Now I've heard everything. Well, I'll be off now. See you, Bentley. All the best, Richard.

(*They shake hands.*)

RICHARD

Look after yourself.

GARY

Don't forget to write.

RICHARD

Give my regards to Simmo.

GARY

Righto. See you, mate.

(GARY *goes out.*)

RICHARD

All right, Bentley, now what's the idea?

BENTLEY

Is he gone?

RICHARD

Who?

BENTLEY

Simmo.

(RICHARD *goes over to the window.*)

RICHARD

Yes, there goes the B now.

(BENTLEY *crawls out from under the bed, looking around cautiously.*)

BENTLEY

I wasn't all that keen to see Simmo.

RICHARD

Oh.

(BENTLEY *indicates* RICHARD'S *suitcase.*)

BENTLEY

Going somewhere?

RICHARD

Yes, I'm going bush to sort myself out.

BENTLEY

Good idea.

RICHARD

Tell me, how's your lovely wife?

BENTLEY

I don't know. She's living with Simmo in our home unit.

RICHARD

Bad luck.

BENTLEY

Yes, it is, rather.

RICHARD

Well, it's great to see you. Funny you should turn up here.

BENTLEY

Well, I wasn't going anywhere in particular, so I thought I might drop in.

RICHARD

Well, uh, like a beer?

BENTLEY

Thanks.

(RICHARD *goes out through the passageway.* BENTLEY *looks apprehensively around him. He sees the dangling pie, goes over and looks at it.* RICHARD *enters with two glasses of beer.*)

RICHARD

Here we are. The old Resch's. Down the hatch.

BENTLEY

Chug-a-lug.

(*They drink.*)

RICHARD

Living with Simmo, is she?

BENTLEY

Yes.

RICHARD

I'm sorry to hear that. Must be a bit of a blow.

BENTLEY

Yes. Well, no, actually, not really.

RICHARD

What do you mean?

BENTLEY

I could see it coming. She only did it to spite me, you know.

RICHARD

Oh?

BENTLEY

Yeah, she heard all about my ... exploits, and so she just did it out of spite.

RICHARD

What exploits?

BENTLEY

Well, you know, the usual thing, having a bit on the side. I mean, we're both men of the world, aren't we? You know what I'm talking about, don't you?

RICHARD

I think so.

BENTLEY

We finally had a showdown when she caught me in flaggers with a bit of fluff. 'All right, you stupid bitch,' I said, 'run off with Simmo and see where it gets you. Me, I'm on clover—been fighting them off with a stick. Don't you worry about me, sweetheart.' She was madly jealous, you see. It had to end this way. 'All right,' I said, 'off you go. A clean break. No hard words. Okay with me. Anyway, it'll give me a free hand—that's one good thing. But,' I said to her, 'don't come crawling to me when Simmo gives you the boot. You just keep out of my sight. I'll be busy living it up in the cot and I won't want you mucking things around. And furthermore,' I said, really giving it to her, 'and furthermore—'

(*He leans on the cash register sculpture while making his point. It rings and the cash drawer pops out.* BENTLEY *stumbles, nearly falls over, then retreats a few paces, gaping at the machine.*)

What's that?

RICHARD

A sculpture.

BENTLEY

What's it called?

RICHARD

'Cash and Carry'.

BENTLEY

I see. Yes, it's very effective. Always the arty one, weren't you?

(*He looks around the room.*)

RICHARD

Huh. I suppose so.

BENTLEY

Nice room you got here.

RICHARD

Like it?

BENTLEY

Yes, it's very well appointed. (*Indicating the pie*) That's an interesting piece of work.

RICHARD

Yes, it's from my brown period. I'm quite fond of it. It has a symphonic density which I find rather appealing.

BENTLEY

It's not bad, but I think it needs a bit of oomph.

(*Pause.*)

RICHARD

A bit of what?

(*Pause.*)

BENTLEY

Oomph.

(*Pause.*)

RICHARD

I'm afraid I haven't got any oomph.

BENTLEY

I remember at school you were always the arty one. Always sketching the teachers. Everyone said you had a brilliant future. And cartoons, too. I remember those cartoons you used to draw. Huh. Bloody funny, some of them. I can still see that one of Davo. Sent him up sky high. Remember it?

RICHARD

Vaguely.

BENTLEY

What a laugh! You did a cartoon of Simmo once, didn't you?

RICHARD

Yes.

BENTLEY

What happened to it?

RICHARD

Simmo tore it up.

BENTLEY

Why?

RICHARD

He said it wasn't in the public interest.

BENTLEY

Bloody Simmo, eh? Done any more cartooning?

RICHARD

No, not for a long while.

BENTLEY

That's a pity.

RICHARD

I've been going on too many benders lately.

BENTLEY

Benders?

RICHARD

Yes, I sort of leave home, get out on the grog, sleep in the park, and ... have a ball. Gary found me in the gutter outside the pub and said I could stay here in the spare room for a while.

BENTLEY

You don't suppose that ... well, now that you're going ...

RICHARD

I'm sure Gary'll put you up.

BENTLEY

It's just temporary, you realise. Till I get back on my feet. I've got to find a point of reference.

RICHARD

Of course.

BENTLEY

I knew I could count on my old mates. That's why I came here. I'm going to look around, find Hammo, size up the prospects. I've got a lot of faith in my old mates.

RICHARD

We all used to be great mates, didn't we?

BENTLEY

I'll say. Huh. Times we used to have!

RICHARD

Thick as thieves, weren't we?

BENTLEY

That's for sure. Do you still remember what we used to get up to at school?

RICHARD

Do I ever!

BENTLEY

Hey, remember that last football match, the grand final when Davo got barrelled?

RICHARD

What match was that?

BENTLEY

You remember, the one against Tykeland. I heard one of them say, 'Get the big bloke!' and when the ruck broke up, Davo was flat on his back and out like a light. Little red-headed Tyke got him.

RICHARD

Can't recall that occasion.

BENTLEY

But Simmo got even. Behind the ref's back. That little red-headed Tyke never got up.

RICHARD

I don't remember that.

(*Pause.*)

BENTLEY

But you were there. You helped carry him off.

RICHARD

Huh. Must have forgotten.

(*Pause.*)

Old Davo. What a funny bloke. Remember the time when Hammo had a copy of *Lady Chat* in his locker and we all looked at it one lunchtime?

BENTLEY

No, what happened?

RICHARD

Well, it was too much for old Davo when he saw the dirtiest bit, on page fifty-five.

BENTLEY

I thought the dirtiest bit in *Lady Chat* was on page thirty-four.

RICHARD

Oh. Could be. Well, anyway, it was too much for old Davo. He crept off to the bog and got a grip on himself.

BENTLEY

I don't recall that.

(*Pause.*)

RICHARD

But you were there. You read it out to him. I can still see

you, standing in front of the Honour Roll.

BENTLEY

Huh. Must have slipped my mind. I remember when Hammo had a copy of *The Sex Life of Robinson Crusoe.*

RICHARD

No, it was *Lady Chat.*

BENTLEY

Funny, I must have forgotten all about it.

(*Pause.*)

Hey, I tell you what I do remember, the night Susan went off.

RICHARD

Susan?

BENTLEY

Yeah. She went off like a rocket.

RICHARD

You must have the wrong one. Susan was a lovely girl. She never dropped her tweeds for anyone, not even Simmo. She had the tightest quim in the whole school.

BENTLEY

I've got news for you, mate.

RICHARD

What?

BENTLEY

Simmo had her that night at the last school dance. They had a pump in the bike shed.

RICHARD

How do you know?

BENTLEY

How do I know? I walked in on them, mate.

RICHARD

And Simmo was ...

BENTLEY

(*nodding*) Chock-a-block.

(*Pause.*)

RICHARD

(*lamely*) Bulls. Susan wouldn't do a thing like that. She was a lovely girl. Hammo didn't deserve a sister like her.

BENTLEY

Hammo? Sister?

RICHARD

Yes.

BENTLEY

She wasn't Hammo's sister.

RICHARD

Of course she was.

BENTLEY

Hammo's sister was called Doreen.

RICHARD

No it wasn't, it was Susan.

BENTLEY

Doreen.

RICHARD

Susan.

BENTLEY

Fair hair, long legs, and a bum steer?

RICHARD

Black. Black hair. Long black hair.

(*Silence.*)

Uh, like another grog?

BENTLEY

No thanks.

(*Pause.*)

RICHARD

Bit on the hot side today. Well, not too hot. Bit warmish, though. It's warmed up a lot.

(*Pause.*)

BENTLEY

It was quite cool the other morning. I was woken by a breeze very early. A southerly change. I got up and went out for a walk. There's a park near where I live with a pond in it. A few willows, the odd lily, that sort of thing. I used to swing on the willows years ago. It was great fun. Held on tight, got a shove, off I went. Up, up, and away, you know? Then I'd slow down to a dangle. I used to dangle over the pond and then climb up the tree. But when I tried to do it the other morning I fell in. Bloody thing snapped and down I went. Slimy. I got out all wet and then went home to bed. I went back to sleep.

(*Pause.*)

Yes, it was quite cool the other morning.

(*Pause.*)

RICHARD

Well, I must be off.

BENTLEY

Righto.

RICHARD

She's all yours.

BENTLEY

Thanks.

RICHARD

I'll leave a note for Gary downstairs and tell him you're the new tenant. You'll like it here. Gary's a good bloke and his Mum cooks a crash hot rissole. Gary's gone away for the weekend, cavorting in the mulga with the Werris Creek Push. You must get him to tell you all about it when he returns. He's a delightful raconteur, in great demand as an after-dinner speaker. You'll like it here. The tap drips in the bog, but otherwise you'll have no worries.

BENTLEY

That's great. I haven't got anywhere to go, you see.

RICHARD

Sure you'll be all right?

BENTLEY

Yes, I'll be all right. I'm going to see if I can find Hammo.

RICHARD

Hammo?

BENTLEY

Yes. Have you seen him? I overheard some blokes talking in the pub about Hammo. Apparently he's running some kind of business. I need a job, you see. Somewhere I can't be ... got at ... by anyone. I've got to find Hammo.

(*Pause.*)

RICHARD

I remember one time some years ago when Gary persuaded me to accompany him on one of his perennial forays into the country. We arrived at this little hick town around dusk. I forget the name of it—someone's gully or creek. I nipped into the pub for a quickie before dinner and I saw Hammo sitting in the corner wearing an old brown overcoat. He was huddled over a brandy by the fireplace. When he saw me, he jumped up with a wild look in his eye and raced out of the back door and on into the foothills. Kept on running till he reached the mountains. His overcoat was billowing out behind him like a parachute, as I remember. I stood on the back step and watched him recede into the distance. It stuck in my mind, that. I never forgot it.

(*Pause.*)

Well, I must be off.

BENTLEY

Righto.

RICHARD

See you later.

BENTLEY

Don't hit the hops too hard.

RICHARD

Righto.

(RICHARD *opens the door.*)

BENTLEY

Ay Richard.

RICHARD

Yes?

BENTLEY

You're my mate, aren't you? I mean, you and Gary, you're my old mates.

RICHARD

Of course.

BENTLEY

You and Gary, you're good mates of mine, aren't you?

RICHARD

Of course, we're good mates.

BENTLEY

That's ... great.

(*Pause.*)

RICHARD

Goodbye, Ben.

BENTLEY

Goodbye, Dick.

(RICHARD *exits.* BENTLEY *goes up to the pie and looks at it. He pushes it. It swings to and fro. He watches it.*)

FADE OUT

SCENE TWO

Saturday morning, two weeks later. Lights up on BENTLEY *in bed asleep. He stirs, wakes up, stretches, and gets out of bed. He plugs in an electric jug and leaves it to boil. He looks around, goes to the record-player, lifts the lid, pulls out a cup and puts it on the table. He looks around, then winces and rubs his back. His eyes light up and he goes to the bed and pulls out a jar of coffee from under the mattress. He puts the coffee on the table and then looks around again. He turns around, scratching his head, and bumps into 'Cash and Carry', which rings. The cash drawer pops out and* BENTLEY *jumps. He looks in the cash drawer and, smiling, pulls out a spoon, which he puts on the table. He looks around, then goes to the bookcase and runs his finger along the books. He pulls out a hunk of bread from the bookcase, puts it on the table, then goes to the back wall and takes down the curved Japanese sword. He cuts a slice of bread with the sword and nibbles it, grimacing. He puts the sword back and gets the jug, which is boiling. He brings the jug over to the table, spoons some coffee into the cup and pours the water in. He looks around, then sneaks over to the door on tip-toe. He opens the door quietly and peers out cautiously. He sneaks out through the door and re-emerges a few seconds later, carrying a bottle of milk. He pours a generous quantity of milk into his cup of coffee, then holds the bottle up. The level of milk is about an inch from the top. He looks around, picks up the jug, pours some water into the milk bottle, and then holds the bottle up. It is full to the top. He scampers across the room like a villain in a silent film and goes out the door. He emerges a few seconds later, without the bottle, closes the door and goes to the table. He picks up his cup of coffee, sips it and goes across to the window. He pulls the curtains back and bright sunlight fills the room. He winces and shields his eyes. He draws the curtains hastily, with an air of decision, puts down his cup and gets back into bed, pulling the blankets over his head.*

FADE OUT

SCENE THREE

Saturday night, two weeks later. Lights up on the empty room. It is lit by a blue light over the bed, which casts a dim blue glow over the room. The sound of rain falling gently on a roof is heard. Slow jazz music can also be heard. The room looks a bit tidier and the pie has gone. After a little while, the door opens and GARY *comes bursting in.*

GARY

Hey poonce features! Are you there?

(BENTLEY *comes in through the passageway. He is half-dressed. During the scene he puts on a clean white shirt, tie etc., and combs his hair.*)

BENTLEY

Hello Gary.

GARY

Phew! What a stink! Smells like King Kong farted.

BENTLEY

I sprayed a bit of the old Airozone around.

GARY

What's all this? Oh I get it, you're setting up for a naughty tonight, are you? Crafty bastard!

BENTLEY

Well, actually, I am thinking of lowering the boom on a young lady I'm taking out tonight.

GARY

You old ram. And to think that all this is going on up here! This used to be a rumpus room for me cousins Craig and Roxanne when they were kiddies. But you'll be up to a different kind of rumpus, won't you? Eh? Bit of a dark horse, aren't you Bentley. Haw! Haw!

(GARY *follows* BENTLEY *all around the room, nudging him.*)

BENTLEY

Ar cut it out, Gary.

GARY

Gunna score between the posts, are you? Haw! Haw!

BENTLEY

Ar jees, Gary.

GARY

Got some frogs under the bed, have you? Haw! Haw!

(BENTLEY *turns on the top light.*)

BENTLEY

All right, Gary, go easy.

(BENTLEY *goes over to a transistor radio on the table and turns off the slow jazz. Then he goes to the record-player and takes off a record. The sound of rain stops.*)

GARY

Righto, mate, don't have a wetty. Just having a friendly go at you.

BENTLEY

I'm aware of that.

GARY

Anyway, what I really mean is, I'm very pleased for you, Bentley. It's about time you had a naughty. This'll be the first you've had since you've been here.

BENTLEY

Oh? What makes you say that?

GARY

Ar come on Bentley, come off it. It's written all over your face. You've been moping round the place like a constipated ostrich ever since you moved in.

BENTLEY

Well, I've been finding my bearings. You've got to have a point of reference, you know. I'm making a comeback.

GARY

And another thing, too. You haven't been outside the front door since you moved in, and it's been four weeks now.

BENTLEY

Well, I haven't sort of got around to going out yet. I'm waiting to hear from Hammo.

GARY

You ought to get out and about more. Look at me and Simmo. We had a great time last night. Went up the country and made a killing on the provincial dogs. Picked up a good tip from a local turf identity. Just as well, though, I lost my shirt on the interstate trots the week before. Went down the mine. We have a great time, me and Simmo. And the tarts! Christ, it's rife up there in the country, mate. Crumpet for the taking.

BENTLEY

Oh? I would have thought that the unfavourable male–female ratio in the rural areas would have mitigated against it.

GARY

That's right, there's lots of crumpet around. Mind you, Bentley, this is just between you and me as men of the world. You wouldn't let on to me Mum, now would you?

BENTLEY

Your secret's safe with me, Gary.

GARY

Thanks, Bentley, you're a real mate. I'm already on the outer with Mum as it is. She put a plate of rissoles down in front of me the other night and I chundered all over them. Too much of the old Resch's. She hasn't said a word to me since, but I'll get around her. Women are all alike, Bentley, you've got to take them with a grain of salt. There's nothing to be afraid of.

BENTLEY

That's for sure. You've just got to know how to handle them, that's all.

GARY

That's the spirit. Get out there and get amongst it. Have one for me, while you're at it.

(*He slaps* BENTLEY *on the back.*)

BENTLEY

I'll do that, Gary.

GARY

Just assert yourself a bit. Throw your weight around.

Remember, in this life it's up for grabs. You've got to go out and get it.

BENTLEY

I'd like to go out and get it, but I don't know where it is.

GARY

Well, anyway, don't let anything stand in your way. Just keep on your toes and walk tall. What you've got to do is stay level-headed and keep your ear to the ground.

(*Pause.* BENTLEY *thinks.*)

BENTLEY

But that's impossible.

GARY

What is?

BENTLEY

How can you keep a level head when your ear's on the ground? It's impossible. You'd be tilted.

GARY

Tilted?

BENTLEY

Tilted. If your ear's on the ground, your head would be tilted. It wouldn't be level.

(BENTLEY *demonstrates. Pause.*)

GARY

I, uh, see what you mean.

BENTLEY

It'd be impossible to remain level-headed.

GARY

That's a point. That's a very valid point.

BENTLEY

You see what I'm driving at?

GARY

Yes, of course.

(*Pause.* GARY *looks at* BENTLEY.)

Well, I'll be off now, Bentley. Have a good time. Hope you don't pick up a dose or put her up the duff or anything like that. Who is she, by the way?

(BENTLEY *is now fully dressed, with his hair combed. He looks in the mirror, then turns to* GARY.)

BENTLEY

Guess.

GARY

Come on, tell me.

BENTLEY

Diane.

GARY

Diane? DIANE?

BENTLEY

That's right.

(GARY *laughs.*)

GARY

Ar Bentley, you bloody mullet!

BENTLEY

Mullet? What do you mean, mullet? Everyone calls me that. I'm no mullet, mate, don't you worry. I'm riding high. I'm on with Diane. It's all arranged. I'm taking her out tonight and we're going places. I rang her up and put the hard word on her. Turns out she's always had a yen for me. Boy, will Davo be jealous! Huh! He's had his eye on her for some time, you know, but I'm the pea, she said. Huh! Will I be on clover! Boy! Old Bentley's done it again. I'll be—

GARY

So you're a big mover with Diane, are you?

BENTLEY

Practically home and hosed.

GARY

That's interesting.

BENTLEY

Eh?

GARY

I saw Diane tonight. She was getting into Simmo's B.

BENTLEY

Bulls.

GARY

Simmo's taking her down to the surf club tonight. She's going to bung on a queue for the lifesavers.

BENTLEY

(*lamely*) Bulls. Diane's a lovely girl. She wouldn't do a thing like that.

GARY

Simmo's taken her under his wing. He's going to be her promoter. (*Laughing*) If you ask him nicely, he might let you stir the porridge. I mean, after all, you used to bat number ten in the second eleven. You can't expect to go in first drop.

BENTLEY

(*almost inaudibly*) But Diane's a lovely girl.

GARY

That's what the football team reckon. Big mover with Diane! You mullet!

(GARY *goes out laughing.* BENTLEY *sits down on his bed.*)

FADE OUT

SCENE FOUR

GARY *is alone on stage. He is putting up a large banner across the back wall. The banner reads,* HAPPY BIRTHDAY, SIMMO. BENTLEY *enters through the passageway, carrying a towel over his shoulder. He is whistling. It is a Saturday night, two weeks later.*

BENTLEY

That tap still drips in the bog.

(*He sees the banner.*)

What's this?

GARY

We're holding a birthday party for Simmo here tonight.

BENTLEY

Here?

GARY

Everywhere. We'll be using the whole house.

BENTLEY

But this is my room.

GARY

We'll need the whole house. It's going to be a real rort. Everyone's coming. All the Manly surf club and a lot of other beach identities. It'll be the turn of the century.

BENTLEY

But look here, you can't—

(RICHARD *and* SANDY *enter. They are both well-dressed, well groomed and prosperous looking.* BENTLEY *stares at them.*)

RICHARD

Hello Bentley.

BENTLEY

Hello Richard.

(*Pause.*)

GARY

Well, looks like you're the first arrivals.

RICHARD

We're always punctual. Would you like a drink, darling?

SANDY

No thanks. I'll wait till the others arrive.

RICHARD

All right. When's the guest of honour due?

GARY

Pretty soon. Did you bring presents for him?

SANDY

Yes, we left them downstairs with the beach identities.

(SANDY *sits down.*)

GARY

Many there?

RICHARD

Filling up. Davo's there, with Susan and Doreen and the others. Alan White's just arrived. And how are you getting on, Bentley?

BENTLEY

Not too bad. I've been adopting a meaningful stance.

RICHARD

That's the shot. Good show.

BENTLEY

How are you getting on?

RICHARD

Very well, thank you. I'm on the board of directors of Simmo Enterprises Ltd.

BENTLEY

You?

RICHARD

That's right.

BENTLEY

That's a bit of a turn-up for the books.

RICHARD

Oh, I don't know. I decided I wanted to be where the action is. There's no percentage in anything else. What's the point of slogging away on the outer? You've got to get on the inside.

BENTLEY

I can't believe it.

RICHARD

Can't you? Simmo decided he'd need my talents.

BENTLEY

What sort of a firm is it?

RICHARD

Well, it's ... hard to describe. How would you put it, Gary?

GARY

Well, it's difficult to explain, really.

RICHARD

You can't exactly put your finger on it, can you?

GARY

No, not in so many words.

RICHARD

It embraces several concepts, all of which are inter-related to the central core, which in turn is made up of the quintessence of the original concepts, with some allowances for divergences within the framework of the whole.

GARY

That's it in a nutshell.

BENTLEY

Are you a member of the firm?

GARY

Yes.

BENTLEY

What about her?

RICHARD

She's my private secretary. By the way, I've moved into

your unit. It's a very nice place.

BENTLEY

What about Simmo?

RICHARD

Oh, Simmo moved out. He's not renowned for monogamy, so I stepped into the breach. We find it a satisfactory arrangement, don't we darling?

SANDY

Very satisfactory.

RICHARD

No hard feelings, old mate?

BENTLEY

I couldn't care less.

RICHARD

Good show. That's the spirit. Well, I see my old room looks much the same. What happened to 'Still Life'?

BENTLEY

I ate it!

RICHARD

You ate it?

BENTLEY

Yes!

RICHARD

Well, quite apart from the metaphysical implications, it must have been a particularly chunderous undertaking. Tell me, what have you been up to?

BENTLEY

Actually, I'm going into business myself.

RICHARD

Really?

BENTLEY

I'm expanding my activities in a number of different directions.

RICHARD

Go on.

BENTLEY

I've established a point of reference. I'm on the up and up.

RICHARD

Glad to hear it.

BENTLEY

Bentley the swinger, that's the good word.

(BENTLEY *moves all over the place, talking excitedly. The others watch impassively.*)

You know, when I married Sandy they all used to whisper behind my back, but I knew what they were saying, I could tell, mate, don't you worry. They were saying, 'How did a poonce like Bentley ever crack on to a horny bird like Sandy?' That's what they said. I heard them, mate, I could tell. But you know what they'll be saying now, they'll be saying, 'How did a swinger like Bentley ever get tied up with a dog-eared tart like Sandy?' That's what they'll be saying, mate, don't you worry.

RICHARD

Why would they say that?

BENTLEY

Why? I'll tell you why. Because Hammo and I are taking over the scene together. That's right. I'm going into business with Hammo. I'm awake up to all the lurks, mate, don't you worry. I've got all the clues. Hammo's got a going concern, he needs a partner for the next stage of development. He said I was the man for the job and that was it. Home and hosed before I knew it. No worries. Boy! I could tell you! Hammo's got a thriving little outfit, don't you worry. Buying and selling, supply and demand. It's simple. Wholesale and retail. It'll be a snack. Hammo said I could be the managing director and he'd see to the rest. Boy! Are we going places! You hear that, we'll be on clover in a couple of years. We'll retire to Coolangatta and buy a penthouse with nude birds running round the terrace and dipping their nipples in our martinis. Me and Hammo, we'll be sitting pretty, I'm telling you. You just watch me and—

RICHARD

Hammo's dead.

BENTLEY

Huh?

GARY

Hammo dropped dead in the pub last night. We got a doctor in, but he was gone.

BENTLEY

Hammo dead?

SANDY

He died of alcoholism. Too much of the 'old Resch's'. It was quite a pathetic case, really. Went on the metho, slept in the park, fell apart at the seams. They took him to a drying-out place, but it was no good.

BENTLEY

Poor old Hammo.

RICHARD

Yes, I felt rather sorry for him. He went quite mad towards the end. Kept on ringing people up and telling them all kinds of weird and wonderful things. He told Davo that Sandy was hot in the pants for him, but Davo subsequently discovered that this was not the case, and copped a black eye for his pains. Yes, I really felt sorry for poor old Hammo. Mind you, he was always a dreamer. Never had both feet on the ground at any given time.

BENTLEY

No business?

GARY

Business? Don't make me laugh. Hammo was on the dole, mate.

BENTLEY

No business.

SANDY

No Hammo.

(*Pause.*)

BENTLEY

Huh.

RICHARD

Yes.

BENTLEY

Well, huh.

GARY

Yes.

BENTLEY

No ...

SANDY

Yes.

(Pause.)

BENTLEY

Poor old Hammo. He was a good mate in the old days. Always liked a drink. Remember the time ... never mind.

GARY

Poor old Hammo. He was a bit funny in the head ever since that time ... you know ... at school ... when Simmo got him in the playground. I saw him once, down by the beach, on the headland there. He was paddling in a rock pool with his overcoat on, and his strides rolled up round his knees. I waved to him, but he didn't see me. He was flying a kite while he paddled. Poor old Hammo.

(DIANE *enters briskly. She wears an expensive-looking cocktail dress.*)

DIANE

Simmo's arrived. He's downstairs, opening his presents and chatting to the beach identities. He'll be up in a minute.

(*Pause.*)

What's he doing here?

(*They all look at* BENTLEY. RICHARD *and* GARY *go over to him.*)

GARY

Uh, look, Bentley, old mate … uh …

RICHARD

You see, Bentley … it's …

GARY

Look, Bentley, old mate, we've been good mates for years, and I've always tried to do the right thing by my mates.

RICHARD

So have I.

GARY

But you see, Bentley, there comes a time when …

RICHARD

(*gently*) I think he wants you to go, Bentley.

GARY

I'm sorry, mate, but I've got to get with the strength.

RICHARD

You've got to be where the action is.

GARY

It's no good being on the outer.

RICHARD

What's the point of being down and out?

GARY

You've got to get with the strength.

RICHARD

That's lifemanship.

GARY

That's life.

DIANE

Hurry up. Simmo'll be here in a minute.

(*Pause.*)

Look, as Simmo's number one girl I insist you get him out of here.

(GARY *pulls out a suitcase from under the bed.*)

GARY

I took the liberty of packing your bag while you were in the bath. Mum made you some rissole and pineapple sandwiches. They're in the bag. Unfortunately, Mum omitted the condiments, but I put some tomato sauce in a thermos for you.

RICHARD

Don't judge us too harshly, Bentley.

GARY

I don't like doing this, Bentley, believe me. We've always been good mates. I'm a bloke who always does the right thing by a bloke.

RICHARD

Please don't think too badly of us.

DIANE

For Christ's sake, hurry up.

(SANDY *stands.*)

SANDY

Don't make a fuss, Benny. You'll only get hurt. I don't want to see you get hurt.

GARY

You'll have to go out the back way, so you don't bump into Simmo. Goodbye old mate. Have a safe journey.

RICHARD

Goodbye, Bentley.

(BENTLEY *moves slowly across to the passageway, carrying his bag. He stops at the passageway and looks around at them. Silence.* SANDY *moves a few paces towards him.*)

SANDY

We're very sorry, Benny.

(BENTLEY *looks at her. Pause.* BENTLEY *goes out. Silence.* DIANE *looks through the doorway.*)

DIANE

Here's Simmo now.

(*They all gather round the doorway and start singing, 'Happy Birthday, Simmo'.*)

CURTAIN

NOTES AND GLOSSARY

Some of the names in ROOTED reflect the common Sydney schoolboy practice of creating nick-names by adding 'o' to the first syllable of a surname. Thus, for instance, Hammond would become Hammo. First names may be treated in the same way—Jacko, Davo.

B (colloquial), an M.G.B., the 'B' model of the M.G. sports car.

Bliss, Johnny, rhyming slang for piss.

Blokes (colloquial), fellows.

Blue (colloquial), a fight.

Bog (colloquial), lavatory.

Buckley's, or **Buckley's chance**, no chance at all. Derived from a pun on the name Buckley & Nunn, a well-known Melbourne department store.

Bull (colloquial), abbreviation of bull-dust or bull-shit, nonsense. *To bung on the bull,* to put on airs, to behave pretentiously.

Bung (colloquial), to put. See bull, also side.

Burp, to eructate; thus *burp a rainbow,* to vomit.

Chug-a-lug, a drinking toast.

Chunder (colloquial), vomit.

Cluey (from clue; also *to be clued up, to have the clues'*), clever; intelligent, knowing the right information.

Cross, The, King's Cross, an inner suburb of Sydney noted for its night-life.

Fang, to drive a car fast and in an aggressive manner.

Fantales, an old-established brand of chocolate-coated toffees, distinguished by the biographies of film stars printed on the wrapping papers.

Flaggers, in, in flagrante delicto.

Frog (colloquial), from French letter, a prophylactic sheath.

Get with the Strength, an advertising slogan of the Commonwealth Bank of Australia, the emblem of which is an elephant.

Grunter (colloquial), a promiscuous girl.

Job (colloquial), as *in job him, job him one,* to hit.

Kero (colloquial), kerosene.

Lurk (colloquial), a crafty dodge.

Middy, a ten fluid ounce beer glass.

Moral, a, a moral certainty.

Mulga, name given to various species of *Acacia,* especially *Acacia aneura;* colloquially, a general term for ragged bushland.

Neg driving, negligent driving.

Niner, a nine-gallon keg.

Poonce, variant of ponce.

Pros and Cons, prostitutes and convicts.

Put away (colloquial), to gaol.

Quim (colloquial), female genitalia.

Red Ned (colloquial), rough red wine.

Resch's, a popular Sydney brand of beer.

Root (colloquial), sexual intercourse; thus *weekend root,* a casual partner. To be *rooted,* to be ruined, trapped, without resource.

Rort (colloquial), from rorty; a riotous gathering or party.

Rubbity, from rubbity-dub, rhyming slang for pub (public house).

Shoot through (colloquial), depart summarily, clear out.

Side, affectation; *to bung on side,* to behave pretentiously or affectedly.

Spit, the big, vomit.

Strides (colloquial), trousers.

Super (colloquial), superannuation benefits.

Turn (colloquial), a party, a formal gathering.

Unit, home unit, a small apartment.

Werris Creek, a country town in north-western New South Wales.

ABOUT THE AUTHOR

Alexander Buzo was born in Sydney in 1944, the son of a civil engineer and a teacher. He was brought up in Armidale, New South Wales, and educated at the Armidale School and later at the International School of Geneva. In 1965 he graduated BA from the University of New South Wales.

After a workshop production of his first play at the New Theatre, Sydney, in 1967, he came to the notice of a national public in 1968 when the Old Tote Theatre Company presented his one-act play *Norm and Ahmed.* This was followed by *Rooted* (1969), *The Front Room Boys* (1969) and *The Roy Murphy Show* (1970). *Rooted* had its first American production with the Hartford State Company in 1972 and its English premiere at the Hampstead Theatre Club in 1973.

In 1972–73 Alexander Buzo was resident playwright with the Melbourne Theatre Company, who presented the first productions of *Macquarie, Tom* and an adaptation from Ibsen, *Batman's Beach-Head. Tom* and *Macquarie* were awarded the Australian Literature Society's gold medal for the best work by an Australian writer in 1972.

Coralie Lansdowne Says No was first performed at the Adelaide Festival in 1974, after which it was seen nationally. It was followed by *Martello Towers* (1976) and *Makassar Reef* (1978). His most recent play, *Big River,* will have its premiere at the 1980 Adelaide Festival.

Alexander Buzo lives in Sydney with his wife and two daughters.

COPYRIGHT

First published in 1973 by Currency Methuen Drama

This edition published in 2021 by Ligature Pty Limited
34 Campbell St · Balmain NSW 2041 · Australia
www.ligatu.re · mail@ligatu.re

e-book ISBN: 9781922749017

ligature *un*tapped

This print edition published in collaboration with Brio Books, an imprint of Booktopia Group Ltd

Level 6, 1A Homebush Bay Drive · Rhodes NSW 2138 · Australia

Print ISBN: 9781761280634

briobooks.com.au

The paper in this book is FSC® certified.
FSC® promotes environmentally responsible, socially beneficial and economically viable management of the world's forests.